Songs & Poems

with Love, from Love, for Love

Luke William Boylan Jones

Contents

Introduction

This is a collection of songs, lyrics, and poems that I composed in a period of peace and tranquility in my life, inspired by my journey and by finding my true love, my soul mate, my one. It was a period of bliss, clarity, and enjoyment gifted to me by so many amazing people and many experiences, both testing and wonderful, spiritual and physical. All of this led me to where I was at the time of writing and where I continue to be now. I have written each of the songs with my own melody in mind, but I would be thankful to hear them sung by anyone who wishes to sing them, with their own melody. You may wish to cut out words, sentences, or sections to fit your song, and you have my complete blessing in that endeavour. We all are living our own song. I hope that some of the words contained in these verses can help you find your voice and sing.

My Journey

A little bit about my journey. My parents were both teachers in comprehensive schools in South East London. They impressed on me from a young age that they were both Atheists and, with the great disparity in Lewisham and the world at the time, I quickly committed to my core beliefs the idea that there was nothing more to believe in than what we could prove. How could there be a God with the amount of disparity and pain that coursed through life? If something could not be clearly explained and proven, then it should not be believed. This line of thinking closed me off to anything outside the physical, and this is where I stayed long in to my twenties.

I decided at the age of 8 that I didn't believe in the conventional system of going to school, college, and university to then get a career that would finally allow you freedom in retirement in your sixties, restricted by the limitations of whatever pension you had managed to obtain and your state of health at that time. I decided that what I was doing, be it education or a career, was not what I wanted to spend my time doing. I wanted to be free from any imposed requirements and until I was I was, trapped focusing on other people's agendas. As such, I didn't care what I did to free myself from it. Any time I spent until I obtained freedom was wasted, so what I was doing was irrelevant. The only focus was spending my time doing whatever would get me to freedom quickest. I would happily clean toilets if that was the most efficient use of my time to achieve this goal. I set the firm belief at that young age that I would retire at 30. I did not know how, but I believed I would. This belief carried on throughout my life as a firm conviction. I wanted to get to 30 and be free from restrictions on my time so I could give myself to the world and help in any way I could.

I had a massive amount of drive, and I set up my first company at 21. I lost this business in 2007, when the recession hit the UK. This was shortly after my son Lee was born. He taught me a massive lesson in life. Although it was extremely daunting for a 20 year old, this was the first step on my spiritual path. Before having him, I had massive aspirations for what I wanted to achieve and what I believed success to be, but in holding him in my arms, I realised that I now had something that I would not trade for any wish I could have previously dreamt up. I would rather spend the rest of my life on benefits and have him than have every success imaginable and be without him. I did, however, go into quite severe depression at this stage. This was due to a massive shift in my understanding. My sub-conscious beliefs about what would make me happy and what life was all about were completely upended. I was not happy in any area of my life. All of my friends stopped spending time with me (other than one, who will always remain my greatest friend for sticking with me through this time). I lost all drive. I lost my business. I was unhappy in my relationship. I was surrounded by a darkness that can only be understood if you have gone through it. It was at this time that, after hitting rock bottom, I met my business partner, Lyndon. He was an inspiration to me. Successful, kind, and a young father like me. He showed me the law of attraction, which I previously would have completely disregarded. Because I looked up to him and had nowhere else to go, I took to the logic that knowing what you want and going into each day with the firm belief that you will get there can only make you more productive. It's certainly more productive than being negative and having no belief in anything. I opened myself up to opportunities and followed synchronicities, and I quickly found myself achieving list after list of my desires. I held onto the optimistic belief that everything that was happening needed to happen to get me to achieve my goals in the quickest, most efficient way. I let go of the negative assumptions I would have made previously. Let me be clear that just imagining something and focusing on it will not bring it to you, as you will never truly believe it will, but asserting yourself each day with optimism will allow you to build momentum, and your belief and success in achieving those things will grow. The more you achieve the more you believe, and the more you believe the more you achieve. Even when our first client screwed us over and refused to pay us the £86,000 he owed us after 4 months of work. This was when I was going into massive debt each month with a young son and was working roughly 60 hours a week.

It was at this time that I took the second step on my spiritual path, although I wasn't aware I was on any path at this stage.

Knowing the situation, Lyndon's nan called me from Trinidad and spoke to me. I had never met her, but I immediately felt connected to her and completely calm and peaceful. She said one thing to me, "Forgive every-body." I was enraged by what had happened and, being in that low state, could only focus on wanting justice, but in that moment, I completely let go of all resentment. In that moment I forgave. Not just him, but every-body and everything. Doing this allowed me to forgive myself, both con-sciously and subconsciously, for all judgements I had made against my-self throughout life. This was freedom. A weight lifted off me, and I was granted a seed of clarity that has grown and flourished ever since. The business became successful, I built an amazing group of friends. I could work when I pleased, I had enough money to do whatever I wanted to and to help those I loved too. I travelled the world having the most amaz-ing experiences life had to offer. I helped thousands of people in various ways. Family, friends, clients, and staff. I had already reproduced and had my son and was quite content in being single at the time.

After achieving one after another of my desires and exceeding every ex-pectation I set myself, I came to a stage of unrest. For the first time in my life I had opened up to the belief that there is more to life than what we can prove. I felt unsettled. There must be more than this. I had achieved everything I had ever wanted, but I still felt a hole inside me. It was at this stage that I realised that I needed to seek more. I started to read spiritual books and research different teachings from around the world. I imple-mented various methods and practices and saw how they impacted my life. What worked and resonated with me, and what didn't. I opened my-self up to the potential of anything. I finally understood that what you know is tiny compared to what you don't know, but that what you don't know you don't know is beyond comprehension. Everything from one side of the universe to the other, which may be finite or may be infinite (either way is bigger than we can comprehend), is knowable information, so what we have discovered so far here on Earth in terms of what has been proven is insignificant, to say the least. Science is constantly disproving what was previously considered as fact due to new methods of testing or new understandings. What does anyone really know? There are plenty of things that you think you know, but how many things do you really know? How many things would you bet your child's life on? I'm guessing not a lot. In opening myself up, I began having experiences that pro-foundly changed my views and beliefs. It wasn't until I was open to having these experiences that I was able to experience them. In 2015, I met my now wife Sophie. I can only explain the moment I saw her as a download of souls. It was as if my hectic world had frozen, a light ran through me, and I instantly knew her. Not just her in the physical, but the depth of her soul. Love at first sight is an understatement. I had a complete knowledge that we were meant to be together. It was as if we had been together throughout many lifetimes and now I had finally found her in this one. Although at this time I was not open to the belief of past lives, my journey and experiences with past life regressions have led me to now have a complete belief in them. After spending nearly two years wrapped up in love with Sophie and enjoying my various successes in life, I had forgotten about my previous belief that I would retire at 30. It was to my complete surprise that 3 months before my 30th birthday, my business partner sat me down in the Hilton in Dartford where we first met and offered me the chance to retire from the business. He knew that I had never been materialistic or chased extreme wealth, that having enough to be free was always enough for me. He explained that he had never seen me as happy as he saw me now and that although he had bigger goals for where he wanted the business to go, to ask me commit to continuing it was unfair. It was then that I realised that that firm belief that was set into my subconscious had materialised. Three months before my 30th birthday, I retired. What you truly believe will be. Not just a conscious belief that you set, but a deep seeded belief on every level. For my 30th birthday present, he treated me to an ayahuasca ceremony in Saratoga Springs. It was the first of my experiences with ayahuasca and spiritual ceremonies and medicines. It was only at this stage on my path that I was ready and open enough for this experience. It was explained to me that in the ceremony, you either go in with an ailment you want to heal or a question you want to answer. As I had nothing I felt I needed to heal, I went in with one question. What is the greatest use of my time for the highest good for all? It was a profound experience. After my second drink, I went outside into a beautiful garden and looked up at the sun. I felt compelled to ask my question. To my complete surprise, a voice spoke back to me, saying just one word. Teach. This was not the voice of my conscience, but a voice external to me that I had never heard before. I felt a complete connection to everything. The Sun, the Earth, the flowers, the mountains, the sea, the animals and insects –. everything. I did not understand how I would teach or in what way. I had never thought about teaching in any form at this point, outside of in my role as an employer. Since then, I have had many spiritual experiences and have taken on many teaching roles and processes that have lead me to where I am currently. I have spent two weeks in the Amazon with a Shaman, been to various retreats around the world, held alternative medicine clinics at my home in Liverpool, and witnessed incredible things. I have passed on experiences at times that felt right, and I've learnt an incredible amount in the process. These songs and poems have been written throughout my time spent teaching. They are a channel for me to convey my own experiences. I would never tell anyone to believe anything without trying it out in their own life and each thought I've conveyed was my belief and response at the time of writing only. As with all things, these could change. However, maybe the information here can bring you some parallel with your own experiences, or some of the words may resonate with where you are now. Some are about my beliefs. Some are about my love for Sophie. Some are about my experiences and observations. Some are just giving thanks for the many things there are to appreciate, and some are just general songs about nothing in particular. The songs are in many different genres. Mostly folk, but also rock, ballads, gospel, soul, funk, house, and even garage and rap (showing my connection to my youth in Lewisham). Feel free to interpret them and alter them however you see fit. I hope that you find within them one or more that resonate with you. That you feel compelled to sing or just enjoy reading them. That they may convey a message that you are ready to hear, or just bring some joy into your day. I give them to you with love, from love, for love.

Special Thanks

I would like to give special thanks to my musical partner Matthew Doyle, who helped me massively in the creative process by creating amazing music that helped develop many of the songs, and for putting up with me singing them. We will hopefully be recording some of the songs and re-leasing them in due course.

I would also like to thank my very close friend Lyndon Modeste, whose help and support in life and business gifted me the freedom of time to focus on writing and music. Also Kadir, Danny, Courtney, James, Fran, and Sydney, who listened regularly to Matt and I perform many of the songs contained and gave us their love, support, and encouragement. Lastly, to all my friends and family that have contributed so much to my experience and journey and who's confirmations and contradictions have helped me to form my views and beliefs.

I dedicate this, my first book, to Sophie, my wife, my inspiration, and my muse. Thank you for being all that you are and continue to become, and thank you for allowing me to be all that I am and continue to become. It also goes out with faithful wishes and expectation for the highest good for all always.

We Are Beings of Strength

From the withered tree a flower blooms
Inside of me feels inside of you
Harmony on whispering trees
The energy of what's to be
Hums on the wings of a hummingbird
Almost so loud it can't be heard

So stop and tune in my friend

Let's go round again
And blissfully taste the nectar of life
The beauty of imperfection evolving into light
The cycles of progress that pass like the night
And the kiss that lingered on the mind

He is a man of strength
Who does not grieve for what he has not
But rejoices for what he has
Oh! rejoices for what he has

Cocoon and go inside to realise the butterfly
Dance with the wolves on a starry night
Dive in to the sea as deep as can be
And feel the in depth of life's harmony

Get lost in the clouded entity
Stretching your whole reality
It'll send you soaring above and beyond
With the blissful serenade of a sweet child's song

Feel the soft soil under your feet
And embrace the energy from the trees
Don't try to steer the river
Know that you'll be delivered
Flow as you go and you'll see

You're guided softly to your ecstasy

She is a woman of strength
Who does not grieve for what she has not
But rejoices for what she has
Oh! rejoices for what she has

Embrace the souls around you
And feel the love that's there for you
For those that may seem a coincidence
Synchronistically came into existence

Now you have the choices of how you dance
on your path
But know that your path will continue to last
And we'll meet again at the end
All those gone and those present

All those gone and those present

We may spare a tear for the lost
But no one is ever gone for eternity
I know all those dearest to me
Will meet me again at the end
They'll meet me again at the end

So please spare a smile for the innocent child
That's on the brink of existence with a heart that's wild
That nature would never contain
Please see outside of your brain
Instead go inside of your heart
Strip yourself back to pureness at start

What lies before us and what lies behind us
Are oh so tiny to what lies within us

Breathe in the essence of your atmosphere
And rejoice in all that has brought you here

We are beings of strength
We do not grieve for what we have not
But rejoice for what we have
Oh! rejoice for what we have

Rejoice for what we have

Luna Lou

Are you still there Luna?
Taking my time to come back to ya
I know I've drifted so far
But I will never let myself lose ya

When they're looking though ya
Making your way to a better future
I'm just playing my part
There is nothing I won't do now

Never before have I felt the distance
That I'm feeling now
On the edge of my own existence
I'm just wondering how

Can I hold on for you?
And will you hold on for me?
Do you believe that it's true?
That I'll always fight to see

Your eyes
And the way that they shine
Your smile
That will always bring mine

The heart of all the battles still beats strongly just for you
I know your still shining for me
Luna Lou

Are you still there Luna?
Taking my time to come back to ya

I know I've drifted so far
But I will never let myself lose ya

When they're looking though ya
Making your way to a better future
I'm just playing my part
There is nothing I won't do now

The heart of all the battles still beats strongly just for you
I know you're still shining for me
Luna Lou

And when I take you in my arms
Nothing will take me away from you
We'll dance among the stars
And I'll bring you the moon

I'll bring you the moon

Go Inside To Know

If you open up your eyes
There's always so much to see
So many different people's lives
And all of their creativity

You can look outside for inspiration
Books and films and art installations
Different teachers
Different mentors

If you resonate with

They can take you places

You can look outside for inspiration
But you can go inside to know

We're all very different
Although similar in places
But only you are you, so only you can know
What is best for you
And where you're meant to go

You can look outside for inspiration
You can choose and choose and choose again
But if you shut your eyes, still your mind and go inside
You can go inside to know

What works for one might work for millions
And what works for many may not work for you
All interconnected but still very different
Go inside and you'll see your own truth

You can look outside for inspiration
Paintings and poems and education

Different teachers
Different mentors

If you resonate with

They can take you places

But you can go inside to know

Yes you can go inside to know

This journey that you're on didn't seem to come with guidance
But there are guides and some are wrong
Which ones do you side with

What works for one might work for none
What works for many may seem fun
But you can go inside to know

Yes you can go inside to know

Nan's Poem

A thought and you're there
A memory that we shared
I hold that thought and close my eyes
And it's the same memory
And you're still alive

A scent that you wore
I inhale
I want more
It reminds me of you
When you were here
But I still smell it now
And I feel that you're near

I still listen to our favourite songs
And I remember how you would dance along
Although you are apparently missing
I still hear them
And I still listen

We all still drink villa Maria
As if we were drinking
With you drinking here
We can all still drink it
The taste of you
You're with us you know
We know it too

We hold the love for you in our hearts
That we held when in life we were still apart
The love is the same
That will never be lost
You will never be lost

We still hold the lessons that you taught us
And we'll learn from them when we should
We still hear your words when we listen
And we listen more than we should

You will always be with us
You live on in our hearts
And we will always be with you
Wherever you are

Olive Twig

Sun shine down on me
And show me that I'm worthy
Show me I'm worthy of your love

Bring me that olive twig my dove
Show me that you forgive
And I'm worthy of your love
Bring me that olive twig my dove

All that is, is resting on the progression of us
Bring me that olive twig my dove

Show me that there is hope
In this never ending sea
Please bring that olive twig to me

Bring me that olive twig my dove
Show me that you forgive
And I'm worthy of your love
Bring me that olive twig my dove

For that simple olive twig
Will be my true salvation
Send the hope back in to me
And send my heart racing
I know that I've been disconnected
But now I've seen my place

So bring me that olive twig my dove

Bring me that olive twig my dove

Show me that you forgive and I'm worthy of your love

Delayed Gratification

Sometimes we are faced
With immediate gratification
Without a thought or concern
For that which could replace it
There may be instant joy
That will last a fleeting moment
But there could be so much more
If we can postpone it

So next time you're about to take
The joy without the thought
Why not stop a moment
Have a think and pause
For that single thing
That will pass within a minute
Can turn in to basket
With lots of joy within in

Next time you are tempted
By a quick indulgent glory
Think of how it might unfold

Into a very different story
If you can overcome the urge
You'll be presented with a seed
That with kindness, love and patience
Can grow into a tree

Thank You

Thank you for the all that is
Oh thank you for the lord
That I can feel inside of me

And guides me wherever I walk

Thank you for the spirit
That is with us in all things
That plays with me in the sunshine
And makes me want to sing

Thank you for my wife
That shares me with this life
The most beautiful that I've ever seen
A love that is forever green

Thank you for my best friends
That are with me until the end
And thank you for the others
My sisters and brothers

The fathers and the mothers
The birds and all the bees
The endless bounds of nature
The seeds that grow up into trees

We're all flourishing
Oh we're all flourishing
You watch us flourishing
Yeah we're all flourishing

Thank you for the nature
That always finds the way to
And thank you for this Earth
That's grounding all of us

Thank you for the stars above
The moon, the sun and their game of love
The angels watching up above
And my ancestors with me

Thank you so much for my son
At the moment my only one
Always been enough for me
More than enough of perfectly

Thank you for my siblings
That grew with me as seedlings
Although we branch off differently
They have the same roots as me

And thank you for my parents
That gifted me my experience
And thank you my soul group
That may take time to recoup

Thank you for my grandparents
They carved this life for us
Brought my parents to the world

And smile down on all of us

We're all flourishing
Oh we're all flourishing
You watch us flourishing
Yeah we're all flourishing

We're all flourishing
Oh we're all flourishing
You watch us flourishing
Yeah we're all flourishing

Thank you for my yet-to-bes

My fulfilling fantasies
Thank you for my ecstasy
And for the food on which I feed

Thank you again for my family
The ever-growing family tree
My in-laws and the growing pieces
My precious nephews and nieces

This tree that grows in to a wood
The network flows out how it should

See those flourishing leaves

And all the new seeds

We're all flourishing
Oh we're all flourishing
You watch us flourishing
Yeah we're all flourishing

Thank you for the seasons
And for all of the reasons
The continual giving more
And more and more

To be thankful for

Choose Again

I am just a child
Brand new experiences
The conscious brain yet to awake

I feel the sharp pain of a wasp's sting
And fear gets programmed in
I do not realise it was only after
The ice cream on my skin

It is too late for me now
I will always fear the wasp

Now I am an adult
Where did I get this fear?

And then I get to thinking
This is not all that I don't know

Many think they know
But do they?
Do they know anything at all?
If it were a game of life and death
Would they bet it all?

So I let go

I let go of it all

I let go of my pre-conceived beliefs
That were built, but not by me
And I find myself free
In a glorious new game

I am now in acceptance
Of a vast expanse of new beliefs

I sift through them cheerfully

And

I choose again

We Are Love

We are all dreamers
Travellers, imaginers
Flying through realms at our own free will

We are all writers
Creators of our world
Writing our thoughts that we will see still

We are all flyers
Searching deep inside us
Flying through space and deeper still

I slow down the world around
Quieten my mind and hear no sound
But that of my breath in and out
And my universe within becomes my out
I can go wherever I wish to be
Sharing with what would connect with me
Travelling to all that I wish to see
Complete creation, no capacity

We are all sailors
And mermaids of kinds
Sailing endless oceans throughout our minds

We are all spacemen
Space women too
With love at our core we are free to pass through

We are all angels
Guidance for those
That open their aura to hear what we propose

I slow down the world around
Quieten my mind and hear no sound

But that of my breath in and out
And my universe within becomes my out
I can go wherever I wish to be
Sharing with what would connect with me
Travelling to all that I wish to see
Complete creation, no capacity

We are vibration
Energy, connection
Connected with those that rise with affection

We are the universe
Planets and stars
Expansions of creation, the sprinkles of dust

We are magicians
Physics, prediction
You can hear the future if you tune in to listen

I slow down the world around
Quieten my mind and hear no sound
But that of my breath in and out
And my universe within becomes my out
I can go wherever I wish to be
Sharing with what would connect with me
Travelling to all that I wish to see
Complete creation, no capacity

We are everywhere
Below and above
We're all that is
We are all love

Sophie

Her name is Sophie
And she came for me
She is my angel
For eternity

She is my start
And she is my goal
She is my heart
And she is my soul

She is my rhythm
And never my blues
She's my inspiration
She is my muse

She is my sunrise
And my sunset
My already happened
And hasn't happened yet

My shoulder to cry on
And my warm embrace
She's my golden kingdom
My happy place

And I will love her
Beyond how I've loved her
Each day growing
Beyond that before

Me beside her
And her beside me
She is my angel
For eternity

Loved through every lifetime
That there's ever been before
All those before now
More than a thousand more

Her name is Sophie
And she came for me
Souls in love forever
Eternity

She's my alone
And she is my team
She's my awake
And she is my dreams

She is my dark
And she is my light
She is my sunshine
And my starry night

She is my hope
And she is my faith
She is my go
And she is my stay

She is my future
And she is my past
She is my first
And she is my last

She is my princess
Soon to be my queen
She's my furthest reaches
And all that's in between

And I will love her
Beyond how I've loved her
Each day growing

Beyond that before

Me beside her
And her beside me
She is my angel
For eternity

Loved through every lifetime
That there's ever been before
All those before now
More than a thousand more

Her name is Sophie
And she came for me
Souls in love forever
Eternity

She is my priceless
And she is my worth
She is my heaven
And she is my earth

She is my wisdom
And my yet to find out
She is my partner
In what life's all about

She's my reborn
And my eternal life
She's my future mother
And my soon to be wife

She is my one
Sent from above
I'm the most grateful man
That I am her love

I will spend every lifetime

As I have before
Being her love
And loving her more

With all that I am
I'll be trying to be
Everything
That she is to me

Until that moment
When we leave this land
And ascend to our heaven
In love
Hand in hand

You May Betray Me My Friend

Thank you for the fun times
And the joy they brought
Thank you for the hard times
And the lessons they taught

Thank you for the loyalty
And the light shared between us
Thank you for betrayal
And for teaching us forgiveness

Thank you for the love
And for the beams of light that spread
And thank you for the fights
And the tears they made us shed

Thank you for the knowing
That we are in continual
Co-creating in this space
For the highest good for all

No matter where you've gone
And no matter where you go
We will always be connected
In the neverending flow

Although we have now parted
And you betrayed me my friend
Love and lessons remain with me
That will be there until the end

I send you love
I send you light
Thank you for the fun times
And thank you for the fights

Tantra Touch

It begins with arms out stretched
Then bring them in with a "yes"
Hold conviction in your clenched fists
And connect to the deepness of the breath

Focus on what you want to be
Or what it is you want to have
Own your own sexuality
Let the motion amass

Then comes the touch
Let go of your inhibitions
Allow yourself to caress
Like waves washing your wishes

Stroke from your neck to your chest
Allow your fingers to explore
Take them to where it feels best
Then flow up from below your core

You feel the energy igniting
Sensations across all your planes
The fire that builds is exciting
The ripples or travelling flames

Now turn to your one and expand
And flow into them bit by bit
Get stable within your positions
Lie down or comfortably sit

Focus on what they are feeling
And realise that you feel it too
Follow the path that's unfolding
You'll intuitively know what to do

Inhale deeply as you look in their eyes
And breath in their sweet exhalation
As they breathe in the energy you're giving
They breath out more to replace it

Clench yourself tightly as you breathe in
And release as you breathe out
Connect to the feel of their skin
And the suppleness of their lips with your mouth

Then you will know when it's time
Without connecting back into thought
The flow will serve as your guide
Always on the precipice of more

Feel your souls intertwining
Connecting and growing with bliss
Physically and spiritually inside
The ecstasy from each well placed kiss

As you keep locked on their pleasure
Your pleasure will grow in sync
The surges grow beyond measure
Without ever needing to think

You'll build up to your mighty climax
Together erupting as one
And after you'll lie by each other
Inspired by what you've just done

And as the waves settle softly
You look out into the night
And you see a shooting star
Fly silently out of sight

You Show Me Heaven

I lie back and breathe
Lying still just breathe
Close my eyes to see
Feel into new reality

Soon the thoughts drift away
My soul walks down a staircase
Feel the sun's rays on my face
Belonging to this wondrous place

Into the most beautiful garden
That I have ever seen

The softest of grass
In the deepest of green
And all that is meant to be
In this perfect serenity

With complete creative control
Can fly to the sky
Or dive down below

The babbling brook
The wandering stream
More real than reality
Awake in a dream

The freshest of fruit
Available with a thought
And everyone I love
From all my lives before
If they were gone in the physical
They are gone no more
All of my soul group
Better than before

Their own version of perfect
In their purest form
Completely connected
There's no need for words
I can feel all you're saying
Though it may sound absurd
It is in fact the most comfortable
That I've ever been
The enhancement of beauty
The best that I've seen
I dance with my friends
And come to a waterfall
And fly to the top
Then with no effort at all
I flip from the rock
Twist around as I fall
Then gracefully land
Into the deepest of pools

Surrounded by fish
Of every description
The purest of worlds
In awesome depiction
The water is perfectly
Warm on my skin
But cool as I open
And swallow it in
I can fly through the water
I would not call it swim

Then out of the water
And into the sky
Higher than the highest
The purest of highs
Through the wonderful sunset
And on into the stars
To dance with the moon
That brightens my heart

Then back to the garden
To a pure purple willow
Where I see my love
And connect with her soul
A soul mate of course
And the purest I've seen her
But more than the sight
The ecstasy to feel her
In the wholeness of transcendence
A phoenix of love
I summon the branches
To close from above
And give perfect privacy
Silence, just us

Complete comfort
But more than that
The power to turn
Thought into fact
Her in her most
Impeccable form
And me in my extent
Of evolution

All that I desire
With the heaven creates
As if it were dancing
To the music I play
With just a feeling
It flows from my heart
The ending of a place
Never seen from the start

And here I've reached
Perfect Nirvana
And an understanding
That ignites my prana
That all will reach

Here with time
We are endless beings
In the school of life
Learning our way
To a golden sunrise
To the the sweet serenade
Of the endless entice
The blissful sound
And the brightest of flowers
That surround us, all around
Like omnipotent towers
Almighty trees
That grow up to the clouds
And the birds and bees
That dance to their sound

You can feel the comfort
Of the doe in the forest
Or the eggs that hatch
In their well-formed nest
And the dolphin leaping
Playfully in the sea
You can connect to it all
You can feel their beat
And the pride of the spider
Weaving an intricate web
The hummingbird's heart
The flow and the ebb

So don't worry for today
Or even tomorrows
Know that you're growing
And you'll outgrow your sorrows
To an understanding
That will grant you your heaven
Which will be purity,
Sublimity, love, everlasting

Sailing To You

Whirling whirlwinds along the way
Learn to dance, to run, to play
Learn to read and the words to say
Learn the beauties of the day

Take it all in as I go
Different shades of wonderful
Trials and tasks and tribulations
Other people's information

Planes and cars and railway stations
Expanse expanding across the nations
So many routes and so many views
But I am sailing straight to you

I love the earth and I love my roots
But I'm expanding straight to you

I'm sailing, sailing to you
I'm sailing, sailing to you
Sailing to you

There may be a wild jubilee of extraordinary goings on
There may be a whole heap of wonderful singers singing their songs

There may be a wealth of adventures
And plenty of fun to be had
But I can feel my perfect purpose
Is to be your best friend and a dad

I'm sailing, sailing to you
I'm sailing, sailing to you
I'm sailing, sailing to you

When I found you I found it all

My all that is ignites with you
We'll set sail and do it all
And we'll sail on to the truth

And when our children touch this land
They will take us by the hand
We'll follow them on their way
And listen to the words they say

We are sailing
Sailing to truth
And now they're sailing
To be with us too

Angel Like You

You are my one
You are my light, you brighten up like the sun
You fill my sky
I love to watch you spread your wings and then fly

And you gave me mine
I was just a man wanting to fly
Until I found you
And you gave me wings and a reason to prove

That I could be an angel like you
Oh I could be an angel like you

You took my hand
And gave me reason to be more than a man
You gave me love
And told me that for you, that was enough

 I gave you flowers
And would write you songs in the small hours
I'd fly beside you
And do all the things I wished I could do

Now that I'm an angel like you
Oh now I'm an angel like you

We dance through the night
Only joy and love, we never fight
We travel the earth
While I spend time to show you your worth

And all that you are
Shining brightly guiding me like a star
And now I'm flying, flying, flying
Yes flying, flying, flying

Casting embers that are guiding, lighting, firing

Oh

Now that I am an angel like you
Now I am an angel like you

I caught your eye
Across a crowded room at the end of a night
And that changed my life
I knew that moment that I'd make you my wife

And we will give love
And watch the angels come and join us above
And we'll say I do
I'll spend the rest of time in love with you

Now that I'm an angel like you
I know that our kids will be too
We'll all be angels with you

I'll Put Up Your Shelves

I am standing on my soap box
Preaching what I think I know
Trying to pass the message on
Trying to pass the message on

I feel the start of rain drops
Falling on my face
And I can only think of you

Twists and turns taking their toll
The bandstand's clearing out now
Wisps of old serviettes blowing on the floor
Taking my time to get my steps right

I feel the pain of hunger
Growing in my gut
And I can only think of you

Making my way through backstreet alleyways
Fastest way that I can get to you
I am out of breath but I won't slow my pace
Wearing out the bottom of my shoes

Bring me
Bring me to your love
Draw me,
Draw me a nice warm bath

You can rub my back while I tell you my stories
Where I've fallen flat
And tales of all my glories

I know that you'll be there for me
Listening and smiling intently

And I'll make sure that I'm there for you
To do any of the things that you need me to do

I'll put up your shelves
And light all of your fires
I'll collect you shells
And I will change your tyres

Making my way through backstreet alleyways
Fastest way that I can get to you
I am out of breath but I won't slow my pace
Wearing out the bottom of my shoes

Bring me
Bring me to your love
Draw me,
Draw me a nice warm bath

You can rub my back while I tell you my stories
Where I've fallen flat
And tales of all my glories

I know that you'll be there for me
Listening and smiling intently
And I'll make sure that I'm there for you
To do any of the things that you need me to do

I'll put up your shelves
And light all of your fires
I'll collect you shells
I will change your tyres

So draw me a nice bath baby
I will light up the fire
I will wash off my day
And then that's where we will lie

That's where we will lie

This One's For You My Love

This one's for you my love
This one's for you

I thank the lord above
For bringing me to you

The first moment I saw you
You stopped my whole wide world
And broke it open into pieces
And shook it with a twirl

You gave me so many questions
And answers at the same time
You gave me so much self belief
Just saying you were mine

And as we grow
We grow
On and on
Upwards we go

We always think we know it all
Until we learn something knew
I always thought I had it all
Until I had you

And from that moment darling
You gave the world to me
You gave me the sight to see
What matters eternally

I could have been a pauper
From that moment on
If I had you my darling
Then my love would carry on

I've got you my darling
So my love will carry on

We wander through as children
With wonder in our hearts   .
Wonder turns to wisdom
But not when we're apart

You brought it all together for me
And made me understand
That the most precious thing in life
Is not the making of a man

But the light and soul and love we hold
Together side by side
We go forth on each adventure
On every roller coaster ride

And with each turmoil we learn
That it was one we had to go through
To bring us back to our true selves
And to bring me back to you

I'll never be able to show you
How much you mean to me
But I enjoy the blissful trying
Throughout eternity
From this life to the next
We evolve beside each other
And although we've drifted far before
You will always be the mother

And I the humble father
Learning as we go
Excited by the universe
Full of things we're yet to know

Your comfort and your guidance
Will never cease to amaze me
You're the deepest parts of all my love
My ability to see
That all is perfectly OK
And better if we wish
I thank the source of everything
That my soulmate you exist
The perfect form for all my wishes
All rolled into one
The love that can only be gifted
By my soulmate, my one.
Clearing A Path

As I look around I see
Expanding philosophies
The sand, the sun, the sea
A couple walking happily

A man raking on the shore
Asking is he meant for more
He looks up and smiles at me
I wonder what it is he sees

You believe what you like
Those that like to believe
Some don't think further ahead
Than what they touch and what they see

We're all each to our own
Endless variation
That's the beauty of expanse
The nature of expansion

We're all making it up as we go along
Or are we raking it up, what's already gone
We're all creating it, like words within the song
Or is it all our fate? What is going on?

Where are we in this world
And the universal swirl
I have never touched the moon
Although it's there, I presume

Last night I saw a shooting star
I was sure it wasn't far
It seemed close enough to touch
But my hand could not reach up

I lay heavy in the sand
And contemplated being man
What's it really all about?
Will we ever understand?

We're all making it up as we go along
Or are we raking it up, what's already gone
We're all creating it, like words within the song
Or is it all our fate? What is going on?

I think back to office life
Where I dreamt amongst the strife
I knew that life was not for me
But without the pain I wouldn't see

So I then set my new intention
Started on my new invention
I created then for me
A path to blissfully be free

I know that none of us know
Really anything at all
Every theory has another
So really what is true at all?
So I choose beliefs that feel good to me
And I open myself up completely
Embrace the option of some magic

That's beyond what we can touch and see

We're all making it up as we go along
Or are we raking it up, what's already gone
We're all creating it, like words within the song
Or is it all our fate? What is going on?

He's now walking his wheel barrow
Filling it up as he goes
I wonder if he stops to contemplate
Or feel the sand beneath his toes

Maybe he's the one that knows
Feels each breath into his nose
Holds the moment, feels the future
Clearing a path as he goes

Clearing a path as he goes

Please Stay True

Please stay true
Go forth with freedom
Harm no one my love
This is truth
Inside is the answer
Fear no one my love
Here for you

And I'm watching oh I'm watching on
I'll never, never stay gone
You're a part of me
Part of me my son

Please stay true
Go forth with freedom
Harm no one my love
This is truth
Inside is the answer
Fear no one my love
Here for you

You're a part of me
Part of me my son

I love you
Be kind my angel
Move on past failure
This is truth

Move on through the hard times
Salvation awaits you
This is truth

Just be you

You're perfectly placed for your perfect purpose

Just do you
Inside is the answer
Light and ancestors
This is truth

I'm here for you

Bring Me Back To You

These are the days of the dreamers
Conjurers, imaginers, believers
We find solace in the sunshine
We find love upon a wind chime

Anything that brings me back to you
I'm within what brings me back to you

I open up my soul for you my darling
I hope that it's a place that you'll be free
Accentuate the best of you my starlet
To imagine and explore, be you, be free

I hope I can go deeper than the surface
I hope that I can breech the depths of you
In you I've found the perfectest of purpose
The wave that sends me sailing back to you

These are the days of the dreamers
Conjurers, imaginers, believers
We find solace in the sunshine
We find love upon a wind chime

Anything that brings me back to you
I'm within what brings me back to you

Infill, deep still, holding on for what reveals

Waiting to be brought back to you
Just waiting to be bought back to you

I place my trust within the winds that circle
The faith that brings the place back to the turtle
I know life will bring me back to you
I'm within what brings me back to you

These are the days of the dreamers
Conjurers, imaginers, believers
We find solace in the sunshine
We find love upon a wind chime

Everything just brings me back to you
I'm within what brings me back to you

Oh I'm within what brings me back to you

Hold On

Hold on
Darling hold on
Darling hold on to me
Hold on to me

Trust in me
Please put your trust in me
Believe in me
Keep believing in me

Darling will you walk with me?
Please will you walk with me
Be there next to me
Stay here next to me

Cause I'm just out here trying
To be the best man I can be
And that's not for me
No that's not for me

I'll just keep on trying
To be the best man I can be
And that's not for me
No that's not for me

That's because you hold on
That's because you hold on
That's because your hold on me
That's because your soul's on me

Darling will you lie with me?
Will you lie down with me?

Lie down next to me

Lie here next to me

Darling will you feel my love?
Promise me that it's enough
Hold me close and feel my heart
Tell me that you feel my heart

Cause I'm just out here trying
To be the best man I can be
And that's not for me
No that's not for me

I'll just keep on trying
To be the best man I can be
And that's not for me
No that's not for me

That's because you hold on
That's because you hold on
That's because your hold on me
That's because your soul's on me

So darling just understand
That I am just a man
I'm fallible
Oh I'm fallible

Please keep holding on
Just keep your hold on me
Please keep holding on
Please keep your hold on me

Cause everything that I am
Everything inside of me
Is cause you hold on me
It's because you hold on me

And I will hold on you my love
With everything I am
And you can hold me too my love
As tightly as you can

Fine Wines And Open Fires

Oh I've been taking the time
Just to realise
The scent of fine wines
And open fires
Just to get back to you
And the way were
Before all the time
Seemed to take its turns

Take me to our home
Where we can be alone
Where we always seem to make sense
Of the unknown

Oh take me to the time
Where we can take the time
To have the open fires
And the finest wines

Where we get can get back to truth
And just shed our lies
To get back to you
And back to our life
So we can take our time baby
And we can speak our minds baby

To get back to the time
Before it took its turns
That is the time
For which I yearn

I've been taking my time
Just to realise
The scent of fine wines
And open fires

Just to get back to you
And the way were
Before all of the time
Seemed to take its turns

Oh I've been taking my time
Just to realise
The scent of fine wines
And open fires
I'm back with you
And we're the way were
Before all of the time
Seemed to take its turns

New World

I'd like you to think of what the world would be to you,
if money didn't exist
If all that we want would come to us, with the simplest of finger clicks
So now that money has no power for you
With the rest of your time here, what would you do?

When you wake up, what would you do first?
Where are your desires? What will quench your thirst?
Please take some time to picture for me
If it could be perfect, what would it be?

If all of us could picture this clear
Hold these visions as if they're already here
Then all of the love and the perfect existence
Would break itself free from its current resistance
Would have seeds sewn and dropped stones
Creating ripples of creation

If we all write and discuss our perfect ideas
We'll see a world full of love for all its years
For all of us here and all us to come
For every being, everyone

We won't discuss things that we would not have
As we will never give focus to that which is bad
We'll only give thought and concise attention
To the love and peace that the world deserves

I won't waste my breath on what's been and what's bad
We're sorry, please forgive us, we love us, that's that
Thank you, existence, for bringing us here
Our consciousness rises, progress is near

If you start to only give thought to the good
Then you'll find it in all the places you look

You'll find it in the media, maybe not on TV
But with the internet, good news is set free
You can find so many ways that human beings
Are saving our world and positively creating
We're improving recycling and sustainability
Protecting our planet, progressing steadily
All of the life, the great and the small
The long and the short, the tiny and tall
The birds and the bees
The ground and the trees
The sky and the animals, the mountains, the seas
The rivers, lakes and all of the beings
We can all coexist and even better can thrive
Finally living, not just existing in life
Contributionism is a concept that would eradicate money
And free the world from hierarchy
Vertical farming is saving the space
Technology's past where we can travel to space
Medicine is developing at an amazing speed
The earth if looked after gives us all that we need
So look inside and be grateful, imagine and create
And you'll see our wide world will truly be great

You Think That You Know

You think that you know but you don't know
You think that you know but you don't know
You think that you know but you don't know

Step 1, Let go

And if you think that there's something missing
Let go of your thoughts and beliefs
Just listen

Still listen

Be still, and listen

Now it is time to finally meet your maker

Welcome

The Creator
Father, Mother, Parent
The Creator

You think that you know but you don't know
You think that you know but you don't know
You think that you know but you don't know

Step 1, Let go

Step 2, listen

Now you've let go, you're connected in the now
And all you have to do is step 3 allow

Just allow

Don't think, just allow

There it is, all that is
And then there's the nothing
So all that is knows what it is
There has to be the nothing

But now it wants to know itself experientially
So the spirit was created
That is you and me
All that is, everything, animals and trees
Everything is love and fear
It's relativity

And now we can move on to step 4
Experience connection and connect some more
You are all creators so now take the floor
Experience, play and create some more

You think that you know but you don't know
You think that you know but you don't know
You think that you know but you don't know

Remember to let go

All that is knows what's best for you
Buckle up and flow to what's best for you
Let emotions be your guide, they're there for you

Step 5, say thank you

Appreciate and elevate
Say thank you
Run, dance, play, create
And say thank you

Always thinks you're doing great
No matter what you do

So love and laugh and never hate
And choose what's you

Don't take things personally
Let everything that is just be

Always do your best, don't assume and don't judge
Experience, create and love
Learn, appreciate and love

Give thanks, give love, we're love
Get love, give love, be love
That's it, you're love and you're loved
Get love, give love, be love

My Only Wish

All that is has given me
Everything gracefully
And I'm thankful
So thankful

There's only one thing I need
Only one wish for which I plead
I've grown through life from boy to man
Happy as I played and ran
And I'm thankful
So thankful

Blissfulness surrounding us
Feeling like we could touch the stars
And we're thankful
So thankful

There' only one thing I need
Only one wish for which I plead
I'll be me and I'll be at peace
Never perceive ungratefully

I'll be thankful
So thankful

I love all that has come for me
But there is one thing that I need
Only one wish that I plead
You can take that all away from me

If you could please just bring to me
This only one wish that I see
The perfect soulmate just for me
That perfect other part of me

I love the earth and all the sea
But wish so deeply all of me
Could be at peace with my other piece
And peacefully, live peacefully

And we'll be thankful
So thankful

All that is has given us
No limits and all its trust
And we are thankful
So thankful

I'd give everything that I have
Appreciate, never be sad
I'd be thankful
So thankful

My only one wish I have in life
Is to find my one and make her my wife
And be thankful
So thankful

The Way

Somewhere somehow someone will know
Already on the path, just need to go
Know what you want and connect to flow
Somewhere somehow the way will show

Clear your mind and you will see
Intuition sets you free
Nowhere to go but here and now
Your emotions show you how

Just stop now and breath
Easily easily
Inhale exhale peacefully
Quietly quietly

Just stop now and hear the sounds
Feel the touch, taste in your mouth
Smell the scent and see the sights
Go inside and feel the light

Somewhere somehow someone will know
Already on the path, just need to go
Choose what you want and connect to flow
Somewhere somehow the way will show

You may feel like you don't know
Well that's exciting don't you know
Be still and wait for it to show
Urges lead you where you need to go

Quiet your mind and hear your soul
And wait for love to fill the hole
You may not know but soon you'll see
Your heart will guide you faithfully

Just stop now and breath
Easily easily
Inhale exhale peacefully
Quietly quietly

You gota make yourself feel at peace
And hold your faith and your belief
That experience will bring to you
The urge to find what you'll love to do

Ooooh the urge to find what you love to do
the urge to find what you love to do

Ooooh the urge to find what you love to do
the urge to find what you love to do

The Mother's Voice

Listen out for the mother's voice
You can hear it if you quiet your mind
Take a walk barefoot through the forest
And you can feel her from the inside

You are always where you need to be
You always have the eyes
for that which you need to see

You will always have capability
Filled with the essence of divinity

You don't need to see your final place
The end of where you're going
The ground beneath your feet
Is filled with all the knowing

You have all that you'll ever need
To allow you to start growing
As you will see from the smallest seed
The greatest proof of all evolving

Listen out for the mother's voice
You can hear it if you quiet your mind
Take a walk barefoot through the forest
And you can feel her from the inside

Trapped In Depression, Freed By Love

Wait for me because I need you to
Wait for me because I'm asking you
Wait for me because I need you to
Wait for me because I'd wait for you

I know that I've been distant
And I sometimes seem down
I've promised you it's not you
But I've still seen your frown

You are my one my darling
And that I know for sure
You sparked the light inside of me
A light I know is pure

I know that I've got demons
I hope they won't scare you away
I know that I'll be my true self
If you're strong enough to wait

Wait for me because I need you to
Wait for me because I'm asking you
Wait for me because I need you to
Wait for me because I'd wait for you

Now I've lost many battles
But I will not lose the war
Cause now I know there's a light in me
And I know that light is pure

Wait for me because I need you to
Wait for me because I'm asking you
Wait for me because I need you to
Wait for me because I'd wait for you

And I know I know I know
That I've been in the dark
But you feel that deep inside of me
I'm still a beating heart

And if you wait for me my love
I'll come through for you
I'll beat back the demons
And I'll be your angel too

You waited for me because I needed you to
You waited for me because I asked you to
You waited for me because I needed you to
You waited for me because I waited for you

If I Stand Alone

If I stand alone
All that I bring is the music

And if I stand alone
All that I bring is the music

But together
We can make harmonies
We can make sweet harmonies

You bring your words
And the flow that you've heard

And if I stand alone
All that I bring is the music

And if I stand alone
I press down upon the keys

All that I bring is the music
But I give all of me

But together
You can bring words to my tune
And we can make harmonies
We can make sweet harmonies

And although I've waited for ever so long
Now we're together
We can make a song
We can make a song

And you'll bring your voice
That sweet sound for me
And you'll bring the words

And I'll hit the keys

And together
We can make a song
Oh together
We can make a song

And if I stand alone
All that I bring is the music
That's why I thank the lord
That I've been given you

So we can make our song

So we can play our song

So we can live our song

Autumn Morning

I walk through on a crisp autumn morning
I broke through
Last night

I only slept for three hours
But I woke up fresh
Excited for the day
That's looking it's best

The sky is a blanket of blue
I have fond memories of winter
In New York coming through

I stroll to a yawning,
Morning coffee shop
A lovely hum on a Sunday
A whole lotta doing not a lot

I stroll through on a crisp autumn morning
I broke through
Last night

The fresh smell of the baked bread
A few kind words are said
Yesterday is all that's dead
And we're thankful

There's a cold crisp air
That feels nice on the breath
And the sun shines on me
To put the warmth on my chest

I walk through on a crisp autumn morning
I broke through
Last night

A child laughs across the table from his grandma
I think back to when I laughed with mine
The world moves and things change thus far
Some gone but never left behind

I take a sip of the warm vanilla chai
I take it in as the planes cross in the sky
I remember I'm the apple of someone's eye
And I'm thankful

Oh I'm thankful

I breath in the crisp autumn morning
I broke through
Last night

I broke through
Last night

Give Love

I was growing up on the rough streets of Lewisham
Parents were teachers, did my studies, I was good at them
Didn't understand when kids would want to fight me,
Raised for good, backing out politely
Why the violence? My head's in a muddle
The pains coming through, better to give a cuddle
Than a punch in a fight, or worse a knife
Just a good little boy on the street at night

What is going on? What has gone wrong?
Why the hell can't we all just get along?
What have I got for you? A heart that's true
You only want my Nokia 32
10 out of 10 in every exam
But academics doesn't seem to be the making of a man
Sell drugs, steal cars, and the fights you've had
That can't be the way you please your mum and dad
I couldn't understand it, but I'm standing in it
Don't fear my friends, this is just the beginning

So please everybody no matter what
Don't think that you know what everyone's got
Don't think that you're in a position to judge
The only thought to give bad people is love

The day that it changed
And I started to think
Was when I went to a friend's
Asking for a drink
He was part of a gang
But he was cool with me
We were at the same school
Always on the same team
It was 9pm and no one was in
He grabbed a dirty glass from the kitchen sink

Filled it from the tap and said that's all I got
He checked his cupboards, expecting not a lot
There was nothing! And I mean nothing
Where is your mother bruv? She's never in
Is this really how people live?
You're only 14 bruv you're still a kid!

So please everybody no matter what
Don't think that you know what everyone's got
Don't think that you're in a position to judge
The only thought to give bad people is love

If I knew just how bad it was to be broke
No father figure, just random blokes
Drugs on the floor of your council flat
Go home when you like, no-ones there when you're back
I would have broke what I had into little pieces
And give you all a piece so that you can eat it
I would ask different questions
And not to mention
Give you way more attention
When you're sitting in detention

My parents, bless their soul
They only had one goal
It wasn't their fault that they just didn't know
That the place I was in was as cold as snow

Wanting to give their children every opportunity
While influencing kids in a broken community
Never had bad thoughts of what Lewisham would do to me
It broke me, it made me. It gave truth to me

I would only ever give love cause I was raised by love
But how cold must you be if you gotta steal gloves?
Robbed for a chicken burger by a gang of ten
Share that out take a bite already starving again
I never knew that there was anything bad

Until at 9 years old a kid got stabbed
And slowly but surely my heart turned dark
Lost all of my faith face down in the park
I didn't ask why would a kid do it to me
I just thought they were scum complete impurity
Now I know the truth and for them to do that to me
They could be raised by crack within a gang family
If they don't steal then they don't eat
So appreciate and don't hate those who are beat
No matter what or how bad somebody is
Just show love and think of these kids
Everyone only wants to feel love
And soon when they do they can start coming up

So please everybody no matter what
Don't think that you know what everyone's got
Don't think you're in a position to judge
The only thought to give bad people is love
The only thought to give bad people is love

Maybe We're All Teachers

Maybe I'm a teacher
Maybe I'm a fool
Maybe I'm a dreamer
Maybe not at all

One thing that I know deep in my soul

I want the highest good for all

All there is
Everything
Everywhere
Out and in

All the places
All the realms
All the levels
Within myself

Maybe we're all teachers
Maybe we're all fools
Maybe we are neither
Maybe we are all

One thing that I know deep in my soul

We want the highest good for all

The highest good for those we love
And those we do not know
Those we do not know exist
Because they have not shown

Those that have done us wrong
And those that are lost

Compassion helps to find them
And that's something we have got

We may be teachers
We may be fools
We may be creators
Of waterfalls

Of flowing rivers
Of mountain tops
Of what we are
And what we're not

One thing that I know deep in my soul
I want the highest good for all

I know that I am learning
In this life that is my school
That teaches me the unknown
And we may never know it all
It teaches me to love
And that maybe love is all
I send intention from my heart
And I breathe in from it all

Maybe I'm a teacher
Maybe I'm a fool
Maybe I'm a dreamer
Maybe not at all

One thing that I know deep in my soul

I want the highest good for all

Sense and Sensibility

I won't take you away
I won't steal you away
I got all the time to take
So take another day

Do you believe in love?
Do you believe in the possibilities?
The birds and the bees
The endless chatter seems to shatter
Chasing down the shadows
That are creeping up on me
Creeping up on me

And I say
What's it really all about?
Do you mind if we go out and look around
A little bit my friend
Search for meaning at the rivers end

And I say
What's it really all about?
Shall we shout it from the mountain tops
Shout it out
The echoes shouting back at you my friend
Back at you my friend
We'll never reach the end
So let it be again

Do you believe in love?
Do you believe in the possibilities?
The birds and the bees
The endless chatter seems to shatter
Chasing down the shadows
That are creeping up on me
Creeping up on me

And I say
What's it really all about?
And all the space
That makes us whirlwind all around again
We search for meaning
At the rivers end
At the rivers end

And I say
What's it really all about?
Shall we kick up the dust
The two of us
The two of us
The wind is blowing back at you my friend

Back at you my friend
We'll never reach the end
So let it be again

Do you believe in love?
Do you believe in the possibilities?
The birds and the bees
The endless chatter seems to shatter
Chasing down the shadows
That are creeping up on me
Creeping up on me

Follow those birds and bees
Let's keep climbing the trees
Let's keep rolling down our hills
And get mud upon those knees

Mud upon those knees

And make sense and sensibility
Sense and sensibility

Forgive Everybody

I feel fear and I feel worry
I feel depression
And anxiety
I feel desire
And I feel anger
It bubbles up
Inside of me

Then I hear a voice that says
Forgive it all, it had its place
Just let go
And now allow
Forgive it all
That is how

Forgive them for they do not know
And even those that just say so
Forgive all and most importantly
I must remember to forgive me

I let it go
And now it's gone
And now my life can carry on
With love and light and joy in me
That forgiveness has now let me see

I'm now at peace
And full of love
The highest good for all of us
The way that it is meant to be
That forgiveness has given me

What Matters Is We Sing

Have you got a plan?
I don't know man
I'll rub the dirt off on the mat
And have a think about that

There could be so many things
About which I could sing
Let me have a cigarette
While I think about it

I would write about my love
And my trials and successes
Does she wash up yes
And she wears those nice dresses

I could sing about the weather
Even when it looks like rain
I could dance in it if I wish
And do that one again

I could write about religion
Or the spiritual path
The way that we grow
And the lessons that last

I could write about desire
And the passionate fire
That grows as you feed it
And burns to inspire

I could write about pain
Revisit that once again
The trials and strains
Of the beautiful brain

I could write about the heart
The place where we start
The guidance it gives
Like the shining of a star

There could be so many things
But what matters is we sing
There could be so many things
But what matters is we sing

Sing sing sing
Sing sing sing
Sing sing sing
Sing sing sing

I could write about nature
What could be the golden gate to
Understanding our fate yeah
And all that has made ya

I could write about evolution
And finding the solution
What a revolution
The spirit brings

There could be so many things
But what matters is we sing
There could be so many things
But what matters is we sing

Yeah what matters is we sing
Yeah what matters is we sing

Yeah what matters is we sing
Yeah what matters is we sing

Sunshine And Miracles

Rainbows
Sunshine
And miracles

Rainbows
Sunshine
And miracles

Evolving the beauty of the spiritual
Evolving the beauty of the spiritual

You can land anywhere on this land
That's your hand so that's your hand?
Go wherever your soul will take you
Chase your goals and let it make you

You may have been broken
But when you're outspoken
The voice inside can then ignite
And you can hear the roar that your core has given you

Rainbows
Sunshine
And miracles

Rainbows
Sunshine
And miracles

You got through and now your strong
You live on
You love on
You give love
And love comes
You realise what's inside and grow and grow

Rainbows
Rainbows
Sunshine
And miracles

Super shining
Gleaming bright
Thank you for all
Of this life

We love this life
We see it's right
The turmoils that
Gave us our might

And now we're ready
Set and primed
For this time
is our time

And I'm supernova-ing
Through it, I'm over it
Unlimited powers
Flying through the sky

Rainbows
Sunshine
And miracles

Rainbows
Sunshine
And miracles

The cycles we thrive through
That we endure then shine through
The open door that we step through
That takes us on to give us more and more

We believe
And we have faith
In what will be
That golden gate

To surrender
And to accept
Embrace, have faith
Take that next step

In what will be
Blissfully
Ecstasy
Perfectly

Succinctly
Energy
That rainbow sun shines down on me

Rainbows
Sunshine
And miracles

Rainbows
Sunshine
And miracles

The Next Best Thing

A wise man wrote writing is good
Then he wrote thinking is better
A wise man wrote cleverness is good
Then he wrote patience is better

To overcome need is to not be controlled by it
Then you are free to fulfil your destiny
I sit and wait, I fast if needs be
And soon the right path will come to me

My mantra is the highest good be done for all always
Comfort in the moment
That the all knows it all
And I will be guided to the best action to take
In every moment it will be available

Thank you for bringing us
As far as we are now
Thank you for the effortless transitions
And always showing how
I observe the nature that grows so perfectly
That breaks down and is reborn effortlessly

Have you witnessed the smallest seed that neither wishes nor worries
But at the end of each lifetime has beautiful life stories?
Have you witnessed the mushroom and its knowledge in the woods?
It travels underground because it feels that it should

It goes to help the needy, the sick and the frail
Not because it needs, but because that's its tale

You do not need to know how to reach the summit
How your journey will rise you above the canopy
You do not need to see the top of your staircase
Just have faith that what's meant to be will be

My mantra is the highest good be done for all always
Comfort in the moment
That the all knows it all
And I will be guided to the right thing to do
And always the strength to rise when we fall

Tethered

And now we're all seeing through different eyes
Yours is yours and mine is mine
In this world of such uncertainty
Some things are just meant to be

And I'll be rolling
I'll be tumbling through the darkness
Through the harshness
I'll be doing the good work
There doing the good work

'Cause I know you've got me tethered
Tethered to you

We know we're OK
We can go our separate ways
No need for asking or checking
No need for updates
Don't be messing
We know we're OK

Even when I tumble through the darkness
Even when I dive in disarray

'Cause I know you've got me tethered
Tethered to you

There's no place where it will take me
that can't get me back to you

'Cause I know you've got me tethered
Tethered to you

We all see things through different eyes
Different memories

Different minds
I'm gonna be doing the good work
Out doing the good work

And there will be no demise
Truth that cuts through the lies

'Cause I know you've got me tethered
Tethered to you

Always At Our Side

You left us beautiful memories
Your love is still our guide
And though we can not see you
You're always at our side

You're with us in our actions
You're with us in our hearts
We'll finish up behind you
But you were right there at our start

We feel you in our moments
We catch you in our view
We're treading in your footsteps
We're us because of you

We smell you in the air
And feel you on the breeze
We hear you in our prayers
Cushioning our knees

We wonder what you're doing
But we know that you're alright
Probably dancing with the angels
And singing in the light

You gave us so much more
Than you could ever know
And we love you so much more
Than we could ever show

Asking You To Sing

I'm just talking to you
I'm just talking to you
I'm just singing to you
Straight from my heart

And I'm just asking you to sing
So I can hear your voice
All the beauty that it brings
Makes me want to rejoice

I'm just asking you to sing
So I can feel your words
They're so inspiring
The best I've ever heard

I'm just showing to you
I'm just showing to you
I'm just giving to you
Giving my heart

And I'm just asking you to sing
So I can hear your voice
All the beauty that it brings
Makes me want to rejoice

I'm just asking you to sing
So I can feel your words
They are so inspiring
The best I've ever heard

I'm just singing for you
I'm just singing for you
My love's ringing for you
To show you my heart

And I'm just asking you to sing
So I can hear your voice
All the beauty that it brings
Makes me want to rejoice

I'm just asking you to sing
So I can feel your words
They are so inspiring
The best I've ever heard

That voice brings me straight to you
Like the pureness of a harp
It's got me coming straight to you
To give you my heart

I'm just looking for you
I'm just looking for you
I'm coming to find you
To give you my heart

I Call Out

I call out
I call out to the darkness
I wonder if it hears me
I wonder what's out there

I call out
I call out to the emptiness
I wonder if it feels me
I wonder if it cares

Can you hear me?
Are you listening?
Can you feel me?
Do you care?

I cry out to the great expanse
I can feel you
Can't I?

Are you full?
Are you vibrant?
Are you listening?
Are you here right beside me?

I can feel you
Can I?

I call out
I call out to the silence
I wonder if it changes
I wonder if it reacts

I call out
Nothing

I close my eyes
I stop calling
I stop my desire
I stop my feeling of lack
I stop my questioning
I stop
I wait
I listen

Finally

I hear

Perfect Now

It seeks the adventure
It seeks all that there is
Caught up in the vastness
Just longing to live

It seeks the freedom
The heart is yearning for
It seeks the kingdom
It seeks to explore

I'm not trying to be a teacher
I'm not trying to guide the way
I'm always looking through a learner's eyes
With a heart that wants to play

I'll fly away in a day dream
Of bliss and new things to see
Until one day I realise
That the answer lies in me

Still within this vast creation
Never feeling it's enough?
Come from appreciation
Come from a place of love

I'm not trying to be a teacher
I'm not trying to guide the way
I'm always looking through a learner's eyes
With a heart that wants to play

Why do we always ask for more?
Then when we get it, still want more
We will never have it done
So life remains a chore

Until one day I realise
That salvation lies in me
That everything is perfect now
And is growing perfectly

I'm not trying to be a teacher
I'm not trying to guide the way
I'm always looking through a learner's eyes
With a heart that wants to play

Just Here To Listen

I'm just here to listen
I'm just here to love
Not going to give my opinion
I'm not here to judge

I won't say I know how you feel
'Cause that ain't real
If I've never been through it before
Then how can I know
I wanna hear more

Just tell me about it oh
Just tell me about it
You can tell me about it oh
You can tell me about it

You can get it off your chest
Then put it back if you need
I'm just here to listen
It's not about me

Just tell me about it oh
Just tell me about it
Just tell me about it oh
Just tell me about it

You have every single right
To feel exactly how you feel
And I am here to listen
And that is what is real

Tell me about it oh
Just tell me about it
Tell me about it oh
Just tell me about it

Say the things you want to say
We can hear them sound that way
Maybe you can make up your mind
Find the answers you need to find

As to what you want to do
And what it means to you
Can do a lot or nothing much
That is up to you

When you tell me about it
You tell me about it

I'm just here to listen
I'm just here to love
Not going to give my opinion
I'm not here to judge

I'm just here listen
I'm not here to judge
Not going to give my opinion
I'm just going to give you love
Oh I'm just going to give you love

What Does Anyone Know?

And so I'm waiting here
For the words to come to me
That will cast out inspiration
A light inside of me

I'm just sitting here
In the darkness, all alone
Nowhere to get to
No way to get back home

I have felt it before
Pure connection to it all
That clearest of truths
The rise before the fall

There have been so many times
When I thought I knew it all
Just to be taken to a place
Where I know nothing at all

And where I see the truth in that
No one knows with me
All following those false old facts
That others may believe

There's this little circle
In which are the things we think we know
A bigger circle next to that
Of what we know we do not know
But there is a greater circle
That may just never end
We don't know what we don't know
And upon that we can depend

How do you get your head around that?

How far can that go?
This could all be pixie dust
We just do not know

But I feel inside of me
I feel it inside of me

Truth
The truth
It's coming up inside of me
Running up beside me
It's always there for us to see
When we have the eyes to see

And so I'm waiting here
For the words to come to me
That will cast out inspiration
A light inside of me

Even in the darkness
We're never alone
A place we find inside ourselves
A place we feel at home

The knowingness to be known
A knowingness to know
A forward motion that we take
Flowing just to flow

So let go

And flow

Guided through the mystery
Shining on your raft
There is more for you to see
You're getting there at last

There have been so many times
When I thought I knew it all
Just to be taken to a place
Where I know nothing at all

Yet we know nothing, and know all
The climb to the top and the fall
The been and gone and yet to come
The guiding star and the shining sun
The deepest depths and the shallow waters
The eureka that is sent to thwart us

Place your feet upon the ground
And hear the silence of the sound
Feel the stillness all around
The words will come to you

My Love

My love
You are my only one
You are my deepest love
From within my soul

And you give me the freedom
To be all that I can be
To be free
With you connected to me

To run, to fight, to give it my all
And to be all that I can be
To see all that I can see
Cause you'll be loving me

Oh I was searching for you
For such a long long time
I've been yearning for you
Always on my mind

The love that's truth
And the trust and the hope
That they live their best life
Always knowing that we're there

Loving you
Unconditional love for you
No matter what you do
I'll be living and loving for you

We could take our different paths
I'll still be loving you
You'll be loving me too
And I know that this is true

Because that's the real love
Oh that's the real love
The only one that you'd fight for
The only one that you'd die for

My love
You are my only one
You are my deepest love
From within my soul

I want to make this future with you
Nothing that I wouldn't do for you
You've given me something more
Than any thing else and more

You've given me a reason
To be the best that I can be
To love deeper than the deep
And it's all easy for me

I would live without water
I would live without food
I would live without possessions
As long as I've got you

I would fight any battle
I would sail any sea
I would go to the end of the Earth
And further if needs be

My love
You are my only one
You are my deepest love
From within my soul

Live Your Song

If you're always trying to be on time
Then time is beneath you
Instead be in time
And time is within you

Take everything that we have
And evolve it to make it better
Take everything that we have
And let it shine
And that feels better

Live your song
Live your soul
Sing your life
Let it flow

Put all of your beauty
Your hopes and your dreams
In that pretty perfect mixing pot
And stir it as you scream

Oh Yeah

Let your heart sing
Let your heart sing
Let your love shine through
Let your love shine through

Something is coming
And it is amazing
You can feel it in the soles of your feet as they're blazing
You're flying excited
Whirl in the whirlwind
You can taste it if you get your senses to dive in

Oh yeah

Oh yeah

Be powerful powerful
You're beautiful
You can feel it inside of you
Hear it, it's guiding you

Got to give your love
You just got to give your love
You just got to give your love

If my soul was a kite
I'd lose the string and let it fly
Let it flutter let it spin
Let it twist within the wind
Let the storms discover it
And the sun shine over it
Let nature be its guide
All the while let it fly

Feel it inside of you
Feel it, it's guiding you
Feel it inside of you

It gives you the energy
And then you are energy
And then you can flow, be free
Grow to all you can be

And really it's limitless
Cycles of blissfulness
Flow through your innocence
Flow from your inner sense

Your heart is guiding you
To the light that's shining through you
Feel it and thank it too

Appreciate to elevate
Even in the hard times too

Just say sorry
Please forgive me
Thank you
I love you

Sorry
Please forgive me
Thank you
I love you

And let me take the beauty of the Okopokoono
And guide it through me
Because it's love that we all know

To love those around you
And watch love surround you
As we all elevate
We all elevate
To the beautiful fate
Which expands as we create

So blissfully create

So blissfully create

We love
We love
We love
We love

We're love
We're life
Let's thrive

Let's thrive

My Guiding Star

She's the one that holds me up
She's my guiding star
She's the one that brings me home
And gets me off at the start

I really don't know what I'd do without her
I really don't know what I'd be
But with my star shining bright in the sky
I've got that love inside me

It's the only thing I know
That in this world of change
Where time will take us all in the end
That will always remain

Because our love is eternal
Beyond all space and time
It is that which has always been
Like the darkness and light

She's the one that holds me up
She's my guiding star
She's the one that brings me home
And gets me off at the start

I really don't know what I'd do without her
I really don't know what I'd be
But with my star shining bright in the sky
I've got that love inside me

She's the one that holds me up
She's my guiding star
She's the one that brings me home
And gets me off at the start

I really don't know what I'd do without her
I really don't know what I'd be
But with my star shining bright in the sky
I've got that love inside me

She's my guardian angel
She's my hopes and dreams
She's my furthest reaches
And everything in between

I really don't know what I'd do without her
I really don't know what I'd be
All that I do, I do it for her
Because she's right beside me

Because she's right beside me

It's all right beside me

Set Your Intentions

You have the power
It's inside of you
Remember the flower
And the sound of that tune

Set your intentions
For all that you wish
In every moment
Believe that it is

You decide
Oh you decide
You decide
Oh you decide

Now you may be on that river
That carries you on to the sea
But you can decide what you ride on
And build it to all it can be

In every moment set your intentions
What would you love
In the following seconds
And what would you love
In the next hour
Know that it's yours
You have the power

Set your intentions
For all that you wish
In every moment
Believe that it is

Segment intending
Throughout your day

The all that is
Brings it your way

I want to go forth and be happy
Enjoy the moments
And the people with me
I want to rejoice
In all that I see
And when I go to bed
I'll sleep peacefully

Set your intentions
For all that you wish
In every moment
Believe that it is

Now you may be on that river
that carries you on to the sea
There's no use in trying to steer it
but you can choose what you want to see

Take your awareness
And place it in joy
And watch as it grows
Into what you enjoy

Watch as it grows
Into what you enjoy

Our Beliefs

I feel it inside of me
I feel it inside of me
I feel your love
I feel it inside of me

We all have our beliefs
We all have our beliefs
We all have our beliefs
And we believe

I feel it inside of me
I feel it inside of me
I feel your love
I feel it inside of me

We all have our beliefs
We all have our beliefs
It may be the source
The spirit
Or the trees

It may be family
Or that friend to me
It may be the universe
Universally
It may be magic
Or it may be routine

But I feel it inside of me
An expanding tree

I feel your love
Oh I feel your love
I feel it, it's guiding me
It's holding me up

It's giving me strength
It's giving me joy
It's keeping me happy
It makes me rejoice

I feel your love
I feel it inside of me
It's holding me up
Its feeling and guiding me

We all have love
We all have torment
We all have questions
You can answer them

We all have our beliefs
We all have our beliefs
We all have our beliefs
And we believe

I Wish

I'm gonna sing to you
About my wishes
My hopes and dreams
And all in between

I hope we all feel love
And we all feel joy
I hope that we're accepted
You don't have to see my point

You don't have to know my past
You don't need to know why
You just need to feel loved
And know there's always another side

And I don't try to assume
What's for the best
Out of the rise or fall
I just wish
For all to be blessed
And for the highest good for all

Learning's exciting
Finding that new thing
And diving in
Sinking or swimming
And it's ok
There's no right way

There's no meant to be
Or best version of me
Or need to become
That's for anyone

You're already divine

With just what's inside
You're already special
There's no need to hide

I wish we'd all feel free
The way we're meant to be
And we may face contention
To teach us to perceive

To teach us to perceive
And choose what to believe
Be true to yourself
And you will be at peace

I don't try to assume
What's for the best
Out of the rise or fall
I just wish
For all to be blessed
And for the highest good for all

We never have it done
But it's already done
You can run the race
Just to have the fun

We've already won
We're already here
Any created fears
They can disappear

And we can let it be
No one is judging me
There's no need to judge
We can let it be

The wish for all to feel their purpose
And to know that they're divine

That we're much deeper than the surface
And to find their Ikigai

No need to search to be the same
Or to search to be different
No need to try to make you hair grow
It's ok to know that we don't know

And I don't try to assume
What's for the best
Out of the rise or fall
I just wish
For all to be blessed
And for the highest good for all

And all that I can know
Is what feels right to me in the moment
Without judgement or analysis
Is that knowing?

Sending out the wish
For the highest good for all
To experience the bliss
When there is the time of all

Be Guided By Your Wonder

Wisdom begins in wonder
Wonder opens our minds
A wandering soul with an open heart
Oh what treasures you will find

You need to respect yourself
And others will respect you
You need to love yourself
And others will love you

Follow the goals you set yourself
Not limits others have set you
Follow the light within yourself
Not the darkness that's outside you

And know that you can let goals go
They don't need to restrict you
We can forever make new goals
The all that is will let you

Every single problem
Is an illusion of the mind
If you're guided by your wonder
Love is what you'll find

We are all expanding
You're not what you leave behind
You are the constant changing
Of the beautiful divine

Clear Wisdom

And so I listen eagerly
To all the voice teaches me
Here in this reality
To take in all that I can see

Breathe in all of the beauty
The babbling brooks
And the swaying trees
The endless array of perfect colour
The warm embrace
Given from my mother

So take in this
But be guided by
The sweet and subtle bliss
Of the voice inside

Be open to that which you do not know
It will bring you joy and the strength to grow
Don't think you won't gather the wisdom
To never seek is to be delivered

Just listen to the you-niverse
The perfect verse in the you in us
To sing you through your song of life
No need for endless sacrifice

I listen to the voice inside me
I find it's truth to softly guide me
I quieten my mind so as to hear it
The wisdom I find is offered clearly

To want for nothing is to end the suffering
But to need for all is suffocating
Do not pretend to know what is meant

For the world around us and all its men
All its children and all that's living
Can all tap in to what it's giving

Do not think you know what's best
But think indeed of more not less
Think of love and think of joy
And feel the warmth sent to enjoy

Create in this reality
The surface is a gift you see
You feel it through all of your senses
Take in all that's in this dimension

Look inside and feel your way
Through glistening nights
And blissful days

Your gut will take you the right way
To the highest good for goodness sake

I listen to the voice inside me
I find it's truth to softly guide me
I quieten my mind so to hear it
The wisdom I find is offered clearly

I listen to that blissful sound
That guides me through the rocky ground
That takes me to what must be found
That fills my soul with what's all around

I take in this picturesque
Moment of the universe
I give it love and appreciation
And thank my soul for this piece of heaven

I take this moment
And bask in the now

'Cause that's all there is
An endless amount

I listen to the busy cricket
And feel the forest and all its thickness
I go where I'm intended to
The flow that's bought these words to you

We listen to the voice inside us
We find its truth to softly guide us
We quieten our minds so as to hear it
The wisdom we find is offered clearly

The wisdom we find is offered clearly

When You Know You Know

Take you back to the boys' house in Greenhithe
Silly boys chasing butterflies
But he was just searching
Searching searching

He could have anything he could describe
Anything he could visualise
But he was just searching
Searching searching

Tied together on a golden thread
Though it seemed it would never sew
Those words that his mother had said
When you know you know

They would say that he had it all
But to him that meant nothing at all
He was just searching
Searching searching

Two ribbons flying alone in the wind
Secretly woven to a message within
Needed space to let the divine In
To become fabrics intertwining

Take you back to the boys' house in Greenhithe
Silly boys chasing butterflies
But he was just searching
Searching searching

My Sol

My Sol
Shining down on me
I let you in
And you let me be

My Sol
Shining down on me
I let you in
And you let me be

I feel your warmth upon my skin
I let you in
And that's saying something

My Sol
Connected to my soul
You give it all
And you ask for nothing

I feel your warmth upon my skin
I let you in
And that's saying something

Your light is shining down on me
Oh your light is shining down on me

It shines down upon us all
There's no preference
You love us all

Your light is shining down on me
I let you in
And you let me be

Striving towards all your glory

Thriving to all we can be
Could be cut down
Or blown away
Or do we live to grow another day?

But in the moment
I'm living perfectly
But in the moment
I'm living perfectly

My Sol
Shining down on me
I let you in
And you let me be

My Sol
Connected to my soul
You give it all
and you ask for nothing

Soon I'll return to your light
Until then
I face you and smile
My time is not over yet
So you'll shine on me
All the while

And your light shines upon us all
You ask for nothing
And you give it all

Saved For You

Baby I need to thank you
For all that you've done for me
For all you've become for me
And for all that you've given me

And I've saved my true love for you
Oh I've saved my true love for you
And I've saved my best self you
Oh I've saved my best self for you

And although I may have given away small parts of myself
I may have walked through hell
I may have been weak as well

I've saved my true love for you
Yes I've saved my true love for you
And I've saved my best self too
'Cause they are just for you

And my best days too

You make my best days too

And you saved your true love for me
Oh you saved your true love for me
You've saved your best self for me
Oh you've saved your best self for me

And although you may have given away small parts of yourself
You may have walked through hell
You may have been weak as well

You've saved your true love for me
You've saved your true love for me

And you've saved your best days best day too
Just for me as a gift from you

And you've saved your best days too
Those that I've shared with you

Oh we saved our true love for us
We are the only ones that are enough
To make us our best selves
And free us from any hell

You are my salvation
And my best creation

You are my freedom
You're my true love

We make us the best of us
We make us the best of us

Oh I've saved my true love for you
Because you're my true love

Sit Quietly

A man stands tall
Breaths deeply
Thinks conscientiously
Gives whole-heartedly

Greatness in motion
Cutting through the wrapping
Revealing more questions
Leaving revelations behind

Rising on new suns
Falling behind the times
Not checking his watch so much
Not checking out either

Distanced from the mundane
Closer to himself
To his loves

A man sits quietly
And finds the blissful answer that not seeking brings

Here for You

I'll show you the way to love
We watch our footsteps up the path
And it goes on and it lasts
As we gradually let down our masks

Sometimes it's a maze
And sometimes we find ourselves
Swimming through the waves
Never reaching the horizon
But if you turn around
I'll be there for you

Oh I'll be there for you
Yes I'll be there for you

Sometimes we're on a staircase
And we can't see the top
And we can't see the bottom
So many times that we've forgotten

The little pieces that produce
All of our beliefs and our truths
A moving changing of our faces

Different spaces
Different places
And through it all

I'll be there for you
Oh I'll be there for you
Yes I'll be there for you

I'll show you the way to love
And as we wander in the splendour
Sometimes stubborn

Then surrendered

Know what I know
Go with the flow
We're never measured
Free to go

And I'll be there for you
I'll be there for you
Yes I'll be there for you

I'll show you the way to love
You thought it was and then it wasn't
You thought it mattered then it didn't
We went through trends and through distinctions
Just to find we're all searching
But what's missing?
The lists are endless but who's writing

And I'm still here for you
I am here for you
I'll always be for you
I'm always here for you

Forgiveness

I've been hurt before
I've been hurt before
Yes I've been hurt before
I've been hurt before

Oh I've been hurt before
Oh I've been hurt before
But now I've let in the love and the light
And I can't be hurt no more

I've been low down trodden on
And hit to the ground
Kicked out trodden down
And cast out the crowd

Hate grew up inside me
Had to let it out
Oh I had let it out
had to let it out

I've been hurt before
I've been hurt before
Yes I've been hurt before
I've been hurt before

Oh I've been hurt before
Oh I've been hurt before
But now I've let in the love and the light
I can't be hurt no more

Was it all my insecurity
Or was it hate in them
That I perceive
The pain I hold inside of me
The rage I can't hold in

Then a whisper came along
The wandering sea

A whisper of love
And prosperity

Words of the wise

And serenity

They whispered in my ear to me

Forgiveness

Oh forgiveness

Forgivenes

Oh forgiveness is the key

Forgive not just that one
Or forgive just yourself
Forgive just the better off
Forgive just the hell

Reach deep down inside
Let go of fear
Embrace the light

Forgiveness for everything

Forgiveness

Oh forgiveness

Forgiveness

Forgiveness is the key

- whistling -

I've been hurt before
I've been hurt before
I've been hurt before
I've been hurt before

Oh I've been hurt before
Oh I've been hurt before
But now I've let in the love and the light
I can't be hurt no more

Now I'm not saying
You have to keep taking the shit

But you can forgive
Be free, let go of it

Forgiveness is the key
To take the weight of it

So you can sail away

With love on your adventure ship

Play That Music

Play that music
Oh play that music for me
'Cause I just want to hear
The way you do it for me

That song
That makes me move it all night long
That music
Just play that music for me

I love that tune
That makes me move

I love that sound
That gives it all to me
'Cause I just want to hear that tune
That takes away all my blues

That music
Just play that music for me

You got that flow
That makes me go
You got that music
That perfect music for me

You got that sound
Right now
You got that music
You got that music for me

So DJ go on play that song
That makes me move it all night long

That music

And it goes doo da da dee da da day
Doo da da dee da da day
Da da doo da da da day
Da da doo da da da day
Doo da da dee da da day

That tune
That sound
That music
Yeah that music
Play that music for me

Sail Away

Maybe we can find a way
And all the words to say
And I will set the sail
And we can sail away

And we can sail away
We can sail away
Oh we can sail away

Maybe I just like your face
Or just that we're in the right place
It could just be the taste
Will make us sail away

Will make us sail away
Make us sail away

And I don't usually
Feel this urgent need
To run from where I am
To stand up as a man

And girls don't usually
Have this effect on me
That make me want to change
And get in a new game

So, maybe we can find a way
And all the words to say
And I will set the sail
And we can sail away

And we can sail away
We can sail away

Maybe it's the words you say
Or the silly games we play
It could just be the pace
That makes us sail away

That makes us sail away
Make us sail away

Oh I just want to find a way
I just want to fly away
Soar into another day
And find ourselves another place

May The Highest Good Be Done For All

May the highest good be done for all
The highest good for all

May the highest good be done for all
The highest good for all

I wake and wish for the highest good
Joy and bliss
And the highest good

May the highest good be done for all
The highest good for all

I sit and wish for the highest good
The joy the bliss
And the highest good

I hear it in the stillness
I feel it in my soul
I place my feet upon the ground
And I know it will unfold

That the highest good is in us all
The highest good within
And I know that it's within us all
It's from the place we all begin

The love and the light
And the pureness of our hearts
The truth within, that awesome might
That we forever are a part of
Of truth, of light of all that truly is
The love, Divine
The all that is

May the highest good be done for all
The highest good for all

May the highest good be done for all
The highest good for all

May we all find our perfect purpose
And understand our truest truth
May we go deep beyond the surface
And find the light inside of you

It's the good that's in us all
Oh it's the good
The highest good
The good that's in us all

Choose Again

We grow we're born
And here we are
Surviving
Like a shining star

Everything we need we have
The expectation
Mum and dad
Striving to go as far

We thirst to feed
We know to cry
So much we need
Or is that a lie?

How did we ever get this far?

We start to grow
We learn to talk
We learn to laugh
And we learn to walk

Get it wrong
Get it right
Choose again

The information has begun
From everywhere
And everyone

It may be wrong
It may be right
We choose again

Our infant selves

We did not choose
For your beliefs
And your not to dos

If you knew
Would you let us choose?

We choose again

These are yours, you give to me
Parents, teachers, society
You don't know if they even serve you
And you don't know if they're even true

If you really knew the truth
You'd choose again

False beliefs keep us trapped
And real beliefs can set us free
But so much of what I've trusted
Was not mine to believe

So I say my friend
There is no judgement
No one really knows what's what
Or how to be
What we are
Or what we should perceive

So I'm urging you to choose again

Oh I'm urging you to choose again

Every question has an answer
And sometimes 4 or 5
Sometimes a different answer
For everyone alive

Different routes, different ways
Different paths and different teachings
Different splits our roads all take
And many different meetings

So I'm urging you to choose again

Oh I'm urging you to choose again

Go inside, find yourself
And decide who you really are
Spend some time with yourself
Because you'll never be apart

Feel what resonates with you
And what's true within your heart
Let go of it, if it doesn't serve you
And choose who you really are

Oh I'm urging you to choose again

You can choose to choose again

Never Truly Alone

I find my self alone right now
I find myself alone

The love that's still there for me now
Never truly alone

Always part of the all that is
I'm always part of the all that is
Never truly alone

I may find myself alone right now
I find myself alone

The love that's there still for me now
Never truly alone

I am here with myself, still included in it all
So much strength inside myself
Allowed to be it all

Connected to the truth of it
I'm connected to the truth

Happy to be still in it
Connected to the truth

And we will never be alone
No we will never be alone

Because it's there, the all
That we're all a perfect part of
It's in all of us
We'll forever be a part of

I'll never be alone at all
I'll never be alone

Connected to it all, in all
Always I'm at home

Because it's there, the all
That we're all a perfect part of
It's in us all, the all
We'll forever be a part of

We'll never be alone at all
We'll never be alone

Because it's there, the all
That we're all a perfect part of
It's in all of us, the all
We'll forever be a part of

So don't you ever feel alone
No don't you ever feel alone

We're together in our home
Our place
Our perfect piece of it
The all
That we'll forever be a part of

We'll forever be
Oh we'll forever be

A part of the all
A part of the all that is
A part of the all
A perfectly perfect piece

And we are all together
All in it together
All in it together

And we will never be alone

Rise Up Together

If you seek it you will find it
And if you build it they will come
Every question has an answer
And there's an all for every one

Tell the truth, it will set you free
What you resist will persist
Sit with fear and realise it's not there
Watch it evaporate into mist

Oh when we rise up
We rise up together
When we rise up
We rise up together

Oh when we rise up
We rise up together
When we rise up
We rise up together

If you seek it you find it
If you see it, it will grow
If you grow it you will reap it
The wise apply what they know

You only need to know the next step
To move towards the top
It's only a mistake if you don't learn
It's only a failure if you stop

Oh when we rise up
We rise up together
When we rise up
We rise up together

Oh when we rise up
We rise up together
When we rise up
We rise up together

If you seek it you will find it
And if you build it they will come
Every question has an answer
And there's an all for every one

Oh when we rise up
We rise up together
When we rise up
We rise up together

Oh when we rise up
We rise up together
When we rise up
We rise up together

Made For Us By Us

Oh I got love for you my love
And I got trust for you my love
Oh I got love for my love you
And I got trust for you my love

'Cause you were sent to me

Yeah you were sent to me by me
By us by we
Exactly where we're meant to be
Beside you by me

Yeah I got love for you my love
And I got trust for you my love
Yeah I got love for you my love
And I got trust for you my love

'Cause you were made for me

Yeah you were made for me by me
By us by we
Exactly where you're meant to be
Beside you by me

Yeah we are meant to be

You're my perfect purpose
The perfect all for me
And I'll be all that I can be
'Cause that's what I am meant to be

And you'll be being all of you
All that perfect all of you
Next to me so perfectly
Perfect next to me

Oh I got love for my love you
And I got trust for you my love
Oh I got love for my love you
And I got trust for you my love

'Cause you were sent to me

Yeah you were sent to me by me
By us by we
Exactly where we're meant to be
Beside you by me

Yeah I got love for you my love
And I got trust for you my love
Yeah I got love for you my love
And I got trust for you my love

'Cause you were made for me

Yeah you were made for me by me
By us by we
Exactly where you're meant to be
Beside you by me

Oh we were made for us by us
And we are all part of the all
We were made for us by all
The perfect form of us for all

All of us perfectly
Being how we're meant to be
Embrace the truth in you my love
We're exactly who we're meant to be

The Sanctuary

We found a sanctuary where we all can be free
A place of love
A place of light
A place of we

Where all have a place
And all have a purpose
Where all have love
And all have light

Where we're all equal
Humans being
All of that thing that is just within us
Just to be

And we're gonna be ourselves
And we're gonna love ourselves
And we're gonna see the beauty in all things

We're going to live in harmony
With all that is
Find our symbiosis
It's easy if you try

You just go inside of yourself
To see who you really are
And you just be that
Perfect
The beautiful being you are

And then when you see see see
What you have in abundance
Then you can give give give
Give what you're urged to give
Give what you have in abundance

And you are respected and you are cherished
You are understood
We're all just beings being
Trying to wander on through
And we give love love love
We give love to all
Kindness is a gift
That is free for all to give
And we all know that all we all want is to be loved

We all appreciate all that there is for us
And all that there is for all
When you see the truth of it
We are all one
We are all humans
We are all connected
We are mankind

The Most Valuable Gift Is Time

As I sit in my shiny car
I look right, not that far
A man on a yacht out at sea
I do not see what's left of me

A man on a bike sees my shiny vehicle
He wishes he could transport more people

A beggar looks on
From across the street
And wishes for the bike
For his weary feet

Being pushed along
Another man weeps
If only he could use his feet

Another man says "I wish that was me
I'd take a life in a chair
If I could only see"

The old man says
"I would accept being blind"
For he has already
Lost his mind
Just one more year
As he sheds a tear
The most valuable gift in life is time

Look Inside

Do not look left
Do not look right
Look inside
And see the light

For if you look
At those below
You may get arrogant
Don't you know

And if you look
At those above
You may feel
You don't have enough

So look inside
And see the light
And see it grow
From dim to bright

From the starting point
Of gratitude
And a loving can-do attitude
You'll understand your strength and might
And all you love will come to light
So don't look left
And don't look right
Look inside
And see the light

The Flower

At first there is imagination
The creation of a thought
Maybe seen in a vision
Or the symbols that are words

Maybe it's a feeling
A knowing of some kind

A wish that sees the seed
For what will one day be divine
A seed that sits there dormant
In the packet of the mind

And then one day a teacher
Or a teaching comes to light
And a chance or opportunity
Becomes a home for the idea

The seed is taken out
And nestled in the chance
And with the light of learning
Becomes the sprouting of a plant

The teachers and the teachings
Shed the light upon the seedling

And the seedling strives for more

Time passes
As we see it
Day by day
Month by month
And maybe year by year

We nurture it and love it

And watch it as it grows

And then a year becomes a month
A day and then an hour

A minute and a moment

And in an instant
There's a flower

Travelling Man

There once was a man
A travelling man
Carried his world in the palm of his hand
Always doing the best that he can
Scraped and scrapped as he travelled the lands

Hallelujah
Hallelujah
Hallelujah
Hallelujah

He lost his kin at a very young age
Was passed around as he had no place
He held hope and a smile on his face
He had no fear and he had no rage

He's been a king and he's been a slave
Lived in a palace and in he lived a cage

Hallelujah
Hallelujah
Hallelujah
Hallelujah

Hallelujah
Hallelujah
Hallelujah
Hallelujah

Up to the top and down to the bottom
No parents to guide, he hasn't got 'em
No one there that is close to him
No very best friend, no next of kin

But a deepness of self and a light within

And a golden heart that is driving him

There once was a man
A travelling man
Carried his world in the palm of his hand
Always doing the best that he can
Scraped and scrapped as he travelled the lands

Hallelujah
Hallelujah
Hallelujah
Hallelujah

Helped all he could and understood
Showed love where others never would
Did so much more than an orphan should
His heart was pure and his soul was good

Step by step guided from above
He never lost hope and he found his love
An orphan girl, the same as him
Opened her heart and she let him in

Hallelujah
Hallelujah
Hallelujah
Hallelujah

Hallelujah
Hallelujah
Hallelujah
Hallelujah

I could feel his light and our destiny
And felt him being drawn to me
And then that faithful day arrived
We were bought together and it changed our lives

I had him and he had me
The love of his life and a family
He's been a king and he's been a slave
He lived in a palace then he lived in a cage

Now once again he is a king
Living in the kingdom of love within

Hallelujah
Hallelujah
Hallelujah
Hallelujah

There once was a man
A travelling man
Carried his world in the palm of his hand
Always doing the best that he can
A smile on his face as he walked through the lands

The Light Within

I listen to the sweet sound
Of the harp play on the wind
I listen to the whispering
Of that little light within

I hear it say to me
Find a place for me
Oh a place me
Such a place must be

What am I meant to be?
Is this meant for me?
What is meant for me?
Surely I can be
All I'm meant to be?

I listen to the sweet strum
Of the beautiful guitar
That seems to beat just like a drum
To the rhythm of my heart
I listen for that needed part
Of the perfect little light within myself

I feel it getting brighter
As I choose
It keeps on getting lighter
As I choose

And then when
I choose again
The light has learnt
To be my friend

And now I fan those blissful flames
And realise that it's bright again
It finds its place in creation

And shines for all to see

I listen to the sweet sound
Of the harp play on the wind
I listen to the sweet song
Of that lovely light within

Walk With The Source

Oo ay oo ay oo ay oo
Oo ay oo ay oo ay oo
Oo ay oo ay oo ay oo
Oo ay oo ay oo ay oo

I feel the ground beneath my feet
I feel the source, it's calling me
I feel the love come from the trees
And the sun shines down on me

I feel the soil between my toes
Don't need to know where to go
For the journey with its endless flow
Starts with but one heel to toe

Oo ay oo ay oo ay oo
Oo ay oo ay oo ay oo
Oo ay oo ay oo ay oo
Oo ay oo ay oo ay oo

I'm looking out across the lake
Watching the ripples that we make
I watch as they dissipate
Understanding more of fate

I take a walk through the woods
I feel it's love, I feel it's good
I watch the ants as they march on
I hear the birds sing their song

Open mind and open heart
The blissfulness of nature's art
I walk with love and walk with faith
Surrender and appreciate

Oo ay oo ay oo ay oo
Oo ay oo ay oo ay oo
Oo ay oo ay oo ay oo

Walk with the source that's guiding you

Friends

Let me tell you of a boy I know
That had his birthday under a strawberry moon
His smile always gives me a glow
Watch him dancing to his favourite tunes

And he knows that I love him
Yes he knows that we love him
And he knows that I love him
Yes he knows that we love him

Let me tell you of a boy I know
That had his birthday under a strawberry moon
I've watched him come and I've watched him go
Each time knowing that he'll come back soon

And he knows that I love him
Yes he knows that we love him

Let me tell you of a girl that I know
With hair of blonde and a cat at her side
Her smile always gives me a glow
Watch her dancing next to her boy's side

And she knows that I love her
Yes she knows that we love her
And she knows that I love her
Yes she knows that we love her

Let me tell you of a girl that I know
With hair of blond and a cat at her side
I've watched her come and I've watched her go
Knowing the light will be there to guide

And they know that I love them
Yes they know that we love them

Oh they know that we love them
Yes they know that we love them

Let me tell you a story of my very close friends
And the inspiration that they've given to me
The moment I see them my worries all end
Their lives much harder, but are always happy

And I know that they love me
Yeah we know that they love us
Oh I know that they love me
Yeah we know that they love us

Alive Now

So I imagine my days away
Play in the honesty of my dreams
Staring out the window
The end of another day
Reality is bursting at the seems

I'm going to wave my magic wand tonight
Immerse myself in all that is I see
Wearing my favourite jacket with the white pin stripes
Embracing what there is in store for me

I feel alive now
Never better
Any weather
Free now

Take my time
First in line
Believe now

Going to set the world on fire
You'll see now

See now

I'm heading to adventure with a bottle in my hand
Whistling and shuffling my feet
A pocket full of party and a magic disco band
Creating peace and love in harmony

I can feel the calling from the mighty magic man
I feel the vibes, they're flowing out to me
Get on the boat of love and push off from the sand
I blissfully set sail to ecstasy

I feel alive now
Never better
Any weather
Free now

Take my time
First in line
Believe now

Going to set the world on fire
You'll see now

See now

Some come and dance along if you want to come with me
The universe is spinning to our song
Creation at it's finest point of creativity
One and all of us can come along

I'm going to wave my magic wand tonight
Immerse my self in all that is I see

So come on come one
Come on come on come on

Come on come on
Come on come on come on

Come on come on
Come on come on come on

Just come and play along with me

We're alive now
Never better
Any weather
Free now

Take our time
First in line
Believe now

Gonna set the world on fire
We see now

See now

As we blissfully sail into ecstasy
Blissfully sail into ecstasy
Blissfully set sail into ecstasy
Blissfully sail into ecstasy

Just Need To Let Go

We just need to let go
Our depression
Our despair

We just need to let go
Of that which should never be there

We just need to let go
Our trauma and our fear

We just need let go
Of that what should never be here

We just need to let go
Let go of our foolish pride
We just need to let go
And go back inside

We just need to let go
Our anger
And jealousy

We just need to let go
And go back to our purity

We just need to be love
Give love from inside ourselves
Let go of our pain
Let go of our hell

And when we can let go
We'll find the light that is love
We just need to let go
So we can be the best part of us

So we can be the light
We can be the love
We can be truth
That is in all of us

We can be the light
We can be the trust
We can just let go
And all be the love

All be the love

Will You Let Me

Will you let me baby
Oh will you let me
Will you let me baby
Yeah will you let me

The night's only young I know
We've still got so much to go
But you have stopped me in my tracks
Now there ain't no going back

No now there ain't no going back
Now there ain't no going back

Will you let me love you?
Will you let me hold you tight?
Will you let me dance with you?
And go with you into the night

The music's got me on the floor
I'm coming up but I want more
You're vibe has got me feeling fine
And I just want to make you mine

Yeah just make you mine
Oh I just want to make you mine

Will you let me love you?
Will you let me hold you tight?
Will you let me dance with you?
And go with you into the night

Into the night
Into the night

Will you let me be the one
That's still with you when you see the sun
Will you let me take your hand
And go into the night

Too Much Riding

There is just too much
Too much
Riding on this

Whatever you want from me
You'll get a response from me
Whatever you need

Whatever you take from me
I'll continue to make for thee
Whatever you need

'Cause there's too much
Oh just too much
Riding on this

Oh there's too much
Oh just too much
Riding on this

And I'll be all that you need
And you'll be all that to me

'Cause there's too much
Oh just too much
Riding on this

Yeah there's too much
Oh just too much
Riding on this

Whatever you seek in me
Every possibility
All that you need

Whatever you ask of me
The easiest task for me
Whatever you need

'Cause there's too much
Oh just too much
Riding on this

Yeah there's too much
Oh just too much
Riding on this

And for you there is nothing too much
The greatest heights
The furthest reaches to touch
The all of it
The more than what is enough

I don't care what
I won't care what
'Cause there's too much
Riding on this

I'll just show love and be all that you need
And you'll be there loving me

'Cause I am there for you
I'll leave it bare for you
And you will for me

I'll continue to care for you
I'll always be there for you
As you will for me

Piece Of Happiness

Sailing away
Flying away
All to find a little piece of happiness

Would you like to sail away with me my love?
So we can find a little piece of happiness
A little space that really doesn't have to be much
A little piece of peace that gives us happiness

It's the only dream of mine
To take my queen away to find
A blissful little piece of love
That we can go and hide behind

And say goodbye to all of our troubles
So she can see just how much I love her

Oh she can see just how much I love her

Would you like to fly away with me my love?
So we can find a little piece of happiness
We'll soar up in to the sky if needs be my love
And find our piece of peace to bring us happiness

It's the only dream of mine
To take my queen away to find
A blissful little piece of love
That we can go and hide behind

And say goodbye to all our troubles
So she can see just how much I love her

Would you like to take a walk with me love
Hand in hand we'll go to find our happiness
Would you like to dream and talk with me my love

And wish upon a star just for our happiness

I would travel to
The ends of the earth
To find the thing that to me
Is of the highest worth

Our very own perfect piece of happiness

Oh it's the only dream of mine
I've found my queen for all of time
And life now just seems so sublime
Now that we are living in our happiness

Sunrise To Sunset

Sunrise
To sunset
Sunrise to sunset

For happiness and health we all strive
To procreate and to feel alive
To search for meaning and the reasons why
Are we all for real or is it synthesised?

Would we know the light with out the shade?
If there was no night would we know the days?
If we didn't have spite would we ever have praise?
Who knows what's right when there's so many ways?

Sunrise
To sunset
Already happened
And hasn't happened yet

We're all on this wheel of life
Ups and downs
Lows and highs

For love, light and honour I live
To be a good father to my kids
To be a good husband to my wife
To be humble but successful in life

Are we seeking the truth or are we following plans?
Was this all meant to be or is it all just chance?
Is it all destiny or is it in our own hands?
I keep learning more but never understand

Sunrise
To sunset

Sunrise to sunset
No lies no regrets

We're all on this wheel of life
Ups and downs
Lows and highs
Hold your focus with your awareness light
On all that you love

And you'll be alright

We Feel Bliss

We feel great
We feel appreciative
We feel love
We feel bliss

We have energy
And we have passion
We have intention
We are expansion

We have optimism
And connectivity
We have understanding
We have ability

We have hope
That grows intention
We have joy
We have connection

We have faith in each moment
For the highest good for all
We are perfect in each moment
That gets more beautiful

We have comfort
We have clarity
We have friendship
We have family

We have love
We are love
We have purpose
Always enough

We have kindness
That we can share
We have compassion
We have care

We have faith in each moment
For the highest good for all
We are perfect in each moment
That gets more beautiful

We feel great
We feel appreciative
We feel love
We feel bliss

My Love

I just want to show you my love
My love
And I just want to give you my love
My love

I just want to sing to you
I just want to sing to you of my love
My love

I want you to feel within you
Feel it deep inside of you
My love
My love

Because everything that I am
My want to be a better man
It is all you
My love
My love
My love

I just want to dance with you
Hopelessly romance with you
My love
My love

I just want to run with you
Lay underneath the sun with you
My love
My love

Because everything that I am
My want to be a better man
It is all you
My love

My love
My love

I just want to show you my love
My love
And I just want to give you my love
My love

I want to create with you
Share each and every day with you
My love
My love

And when I take that last breath
I want to be holding you to my chest
Knowing that you've had your last breath too
And knowing we've done all we wanted to do

And we will go on to our next adventure
Side by side, still together
My love
My love
My love
And I'll never stop loving you

Where The Time Has Gone

Many years have passed
Many times have gone
Many tears and laughs
Where the time has gone

Hardness facing in to me
All the places that we could be
And I'll be holding on with all I am
You can trust in your faith in me

And I will hold you close when you need me to
And I will give you space when you need that too
And although darkness may roll over me
The light inside you can always see

Gone is the pretty surface
That twinkles in the dancing sun
It lacked the depth that were now in
Yet every moment our life has just begun

Spring turns in to summer
Summer, autumn into winter time
Another year has gone and passed us by
But I still see the love deep in your eyes

And I will hold you close when you need me to
And I will give you space when you need that too
And although darkness may roll over me
The light inside you I can always see

Take my hand now my darling
Let us dance beneath the stars
Let us reminisce of times gone by
Let us cast a wish and fantasise

Now I'm not saying it's been easy
But I would do it all a thousand times
I know you'll always be there with me
Through darkest dark right back to the light

Many years have passed
Many times have gone
Many tears and laughs
Where the time has gone

And I will hold you close when you need me to

Throughout it all I'll keep loving you

Throughout it all I'll keep loving you

Subconscious Review

I've been wondering about
All the wonders in the out
Side of me

And so I go inside
And ride the waves of night
Tackle it and fight
All that's
Inside of me

I stay with each memory
They make me remember me
I respond to them so differently
Another possibility
And
Side of me

Through eyes so young
When life had just begun
I made a judgment
An assumption
Built from lack
Of life's building wisdom

And there they stayed
Inside of me

Made from false rhymes or reason
Made from fear
And then in sank in
Lost within the chasm of the mind

And as I grew
I barely knew
That they were still there

Forming my truths

Who knew
That they were left inside of me

Until I rode the waves of night
Sat with them
And shed new light
Chose again
To my delight
The memories that that would ignite
A beautiful blissfulness
In the life
Outside of me

Living Our Dreams

The sunrise on a beautiful scene
We're just out here chasing our dreams
The sunlight reflects on you and me
We've all got the wings beneath our feet

We just want to bring you joy
We just want to bring you joy
We just want to bring you joy
We just want to bring you joy

Moving on forward to our purpose
Not seeing lack we're seeing surplus
There's more than enough for all of us
Our love keeps bringing the joy to us

Tapping our feet, clicking our fingers
Listening to the sound of singers
Music is playing all of the time
Kisses and shooting stars in the sky

We just want to bring you joy
We just want to bring you joy
We just want to bring you joy
We just want to bring you joy

A brand new coat with shoes to match
A brand new present for us to catch
Rolling down the endless highways
And I know that I've done it my way

We're feeling good yeah we're feeling fine
We're stretching the limits of our minds
No longer trapped no longer confined
Dancing in love, this is so sublime

We just want to bring you joy
Joy, joy, joy
Yeah we just want to bring you joy
Joy, joy, joy

The sunsets on a beautiful scene
We're just out here living our dreams
The sunlight reflects on you and me
We appreciate it so thankfully

Pineapple In The Sky

I love the way you you look into the sunglasses on the table
That show you a golden pineapple in the sky

And it's all about your eye

And what you let your imagination identify

Rather than the need to try
To quantify
The unquantifiable, undeniable
Beautiful, magical
Blissful, lyrical
Rhythm inside us all

Raising us higher towards
All of our future rewards
For all of the love we sow now
The ripples that show others how

From the ground up and out
Helter skelter
Roundabout
All within
No one without

Wizards in a windowpane
Casting spells in times of change
Evolving beyond all the gains
Of our previous loves and pains

We endure what we can endure
To bring us on to so much more
All of which to be thankful for
The love that emanates is pure

Ask if there's more, there's more

Everlasting wonderful
For every last one and all
The journey that has been our school
The heart has been our teacher

And we're finally here to meet you

Evolve to be you

So see you

Very soon

Love Is The Answer

Love is the answer
A hopeful romancer
Love is a dancer
That's happy and free

Love is the answer
To all of life's questions
And you may not think it
But it is the best one

Love is the answer
Love is the answer
Love is a dancer
That's joyous and free

That's joyous and free
That's joyous and free
That's joyous and free
Joyous and free

Love is the answer
An always-takes-a-chancer
Love is a dancer
That's in you and me

Love is the answer
A preacher, a prancer
A giving and taking
Like the tides of the sea

Like the tides of the sea
Like the tides of the sea
Like the tides of the sea
The tides of the sea

Love is the answer
A hopeful romancer
Love is a dancer
That's joyous and free

Love is the answer
To all of life's questions
But what are the questions?
The love says to me

The love says to me

Angel

I have pure thoughts
And strength in my heart
I feel like today
I'm right at the start
So please will you guide me
And allow me to feel
That which I was
Unable to see

I can feel your embrace holding me up
Taking me forward to the warmth of your love
Taking me forward
To the warmth of your love

All that there is
Has sent you to me
To ascend my soul
Into new purity

Give me your patience
Compassion and love
So that I can embrace
All of us

I can feel your embrace holding me up
Taking me forward to the warmth of your love
Taking me forward
To the warmth of your love

You're always with me
I feel you there
Thank you so much
For how much you care
In all that I am
And I'm able to be

I return the love
That you have for me

Thank you for holding
Your vibration for me
Thank you for loving
When I could not see
Thank you for patience
When I was stubborn
To open my heart
And use it to learn

To embrace anything
Other than what I knew
To take interest in the knowledge
That would bring me to you
To open my mind
And open my heart
To go back to the love
I was at the start
To go back to the love
I was at the start

Funky Music

So many people
Trying to tell me how to live
Their contradictions
And agreements regarded

No one really knows anything
So let's just let it go
And let it in

Let's make some funky movement to the funky music
Feel the weight in your body as you move it
Connect to the sound waves
You are tuned in
On the frequency of love and life
Your consuming

How about we stop

Now it's a new moment
And we own it
Don't need to fly the coop
We've just flown in

We can bubble
We can boogie
We can shuffle
We can skank

We connect in the moment
Feel the love and give thanks

So many lovely people, lovely people
So many

Lovely people, lovely people
So many

Let's make some funky movement to the funky music
Feel the weight in your body as you move it
Connect to the sound waves

You are tuned in
On the frequency of love and life
Your consuming

Surrounded by lovely people

And if you really understood each one you'd see you

You'd see you

Do you
Be you
Be kind
Be true
Give love
Have love
Share love
We're love

Let's make some funky movement to the funky music
Feel the weight in your body as you move it
Connect to the sound waves
You are tuned in
On the frequency of love and life
You're consuming

Breathe it in

You're a human

So let's be a human doing

All the things that we're in tune with

I thank you for the love and return it

Don't need to start a fire, we've just burnt it

Butterfly

I climb the stairway to the end
One step at a time
As I climb higher, I see further
But I'm losing my time

Lucky is the caterpillar
Butterfly he now has found
He can flutter in the air space
But lost his place along the ground

He does not miss his past
Or worry for the future
He lives within the moment
Embracing all it's splendour

Promised Land

Where are we going we now?
Can we tell from where we've been?
All the things we're yet to see?
Are we all on the same path to the same place?
To be delivered to the promised land

Now we all will leave the physical
And that's something we know for sure is true
But maybe we will come back again
To live a life of a foe or friend
So maybe when you look now
You should look again

Are we all on the same path to the same place?
To be delivered to the promised land

I sit and stare in to the great abyss
And wonder if there's something I've missed
The feelings deep down inside of me
Of our eventuality
Flowing as we go
Sometimes fast and sometimes slow
Feeling somehow that we know
We'll be delivered to the promised land

But yet know one knows
Where our pretty river flows
On and on and on we go
Feel the earth beneath our toes
Guided by the sunshine
In it we always feel fine

On and on and on we go
To be delivered to the promised land

So many different stories
People spend their life defending
But does it all really matter?
When they all have the same ending

So enjoy every minute
All the blisses, all the beauties
Make your stories and let truth be told
Watch new life and watch the old
Every struggle that we face
Will still take us to the place

On and on to our promised land

We'll be going on into the promised land

Get Up, Stand Up

Now you better take a stand now
You're going to be the man now
One foot in front of the other now
You know you got the love of your brother now
Don't need to know how
We can always make a plan now
Get up, stand up make a stand now

We're going to hit the top now
Never stop now
Fly high in the sky with a rocket now
Now I've flown to the top
The sky is my bottom now
All the things that I wanted
I have got 'em now

But don't stop, never stop
I'll keep going now
I'll build up drop by drop
I'll make a cloud
Then rain down all the love
Give it all out
Make your loved ones proud

If you need to find some love
Just look around
'Cause love is all around
If you can't see it out
Go inside now
See the love from within
Feel the light now
That endless exploration
It's your right now

Now you better take a stand now

You're going to be the man now
One foot in front of the other now
You know you got the love of your brother now
Don't need to know how
You can always make a plan now
Get up stand up make a stand now

There are faces and places that life never seemed to mention
And all of a sudden they're taking my attention
Plenty of options to get some inspiration
Read a book, take a look, maybe visit a new nation
Sit with yourself in quiet contemplation
Ready to hit the world, stand up and put my face on

A big smile ear to ear
I've already made it here
Broke down, got back up
Learnt to overcome my fear

See the world through eyes of love now
So many of my loved ones near me now
See them all coming up makes me so proud
So we're just gonna sing now
Get up and stand up, stand up for your life

Living In The Moment

I try living in the moment
'Cause in the moment
I've got so much to hold onto
Oh I try living in the moment
'Cause in the moment
I've got so much to be thankful for

Yeah I stay living in the moment
'Cause in the moment
I've got so much to hold onto
Oh I try living in the moment
'Cause In the moment
I've got so much to be thankful for

There's beauty in everything
Be unique, keep on dreaming
Bring out that strength within
Time you wasted enjoying
Is not time wasted

Live, let live, help live
Never let go of your wishes
Turn I wish into I will
Be kind, then be kinder still
Happiness is at our will

I try living in the moment
'Cause in the moment
I've got so much to hold onto
Oh I try living in the moment
'Cause in the moment
I've got so much to be thankful for

Yeah I stay living in the moment
'Cause in the moment

I've got so much to hold onto
Oh I try living in the moment
'Cause In the moment
I've got so much to be thankful for

Breathe and take it in
The beauty that's out
And the beauty that's in
Start forgiving and begin living
Nothing can dim the light from within

We are who we are
Believe in yourself
It starts with being you
From inside yourself

Always look on the brightest side
Happiness is something we choose

So why don't you be a somebody
That makes everybody
Feel like a somebody too
The one that fell and got up
Will always be so much stronger
Than the one that was too scared to move

I try living in the moment
'Cause in the moment
I've got so much to hold onto
Oh I try living in the moment
'Cause In the moment
I've got so much to be thankful for

Yeah I stay living in the moment
'Cause in the moment
I've got so much to hold onto
Oh I try living in the moment
'Cause In the moment

I've got so much to be thankful for

No dream is too big
Let yourself imagine it
Don't let small minds
Stop your belief
Anything can be achieved

Look ahead, don't look back
Mistakes give knowledge
And that's a fact
There's beauty in everything
Be unique, keep on dreaming

A Magical Place

I want to take you
To a magical place
Where we can both get lost
In our embrace

And the stars sparkle
Like your eyes under the moon
And the water's warm
When I swim in it with you

We can touch the clouds
And shout out loud
We can dance on tabletops
And make each other proud

We can drink all day
If that's what we choose to do
Others chase the blues away
But I have no blues with you

You complete me
Make me better than I am
Make me evolve
From the previous state of man

You intoxicate me
And you inspire me too
You're my adventures
Darling you are my muse

You're the soulful tune
That plays within my heart
You're my get up
Ready to start

You're the sunshine
That brightens my world
So let me take you to
A crystal wonder world

Where the birds fly right by your side
And wild horses stop to let you ride
Where you can walk on white soft sands
And you can feel my love just holding hands

I will be the man
You always wished for
Because my darling
To me you're so much more

You are my festival
My music and my dance
You are my angel dust
That allows me to advance

You are my love
Thank you for all you are
So let's fly up above
To dance among the stars

Fly With You To The Moon

So I want to fly with you to the moon
And I don't pretend to know what I should do
If you ask I'll give all I know to you
And when the time is right I'm sure you'll ask me too

Oh I want to know
More than what's in my soul
And I want to see
More than what's been shown to me
Oh I want to go
To places beyond those I know
Oh I want to feel
More than what I know as real

We are love
We are trust
On the brink of evolution
Let's not overthink this revolution
Of the soul
Of the soul

So I don't try to overthink
That I can help the universe
I know that the universe will guide me
To all that I should do
I know what's right for me
Will always be alright with you
I know what's right for me
Will always be alright with you

I used to think that I should help
And do all that I can
For those in a worse position
But who am I?
I'm only a man

Who am I to say what's right
To guide us all through the night
We've all got the light inside us
So we connect and let it guide us

I want to fly with you onto the moon
But I don't pretend to know what I should do
I will go forth with love and care in my heart
And we will journey to the future, back to start

Oh I want to know
More than what's in my soul
And I want to see
More than what's been shown to me
Oh I want to go
To places beyond those I know
Oh I want to feel
More than what I know as real

Whatever we all need to do
I know we can all feel the truth
And take us to the destination
That may be stationed
Where we are

The brightest light, the brightest star
Can be unreachable, or not that far
But if we take away our desire
For the warmth of the fire
We will find the warmth inside our souls

There is a goal for all of us
Believe in our souls and they will take us
Exactly down our chosen path
To where we love and laugh at last

Oh I want to know
More than what's in my soul

And I want to see
More than what's been shown to me
Oh I want to go
To places beyond those I know
Oh I want to feel
More than what I know as real

Fall

I look at the sturdy trees
I watch them hold onto their leaves
Until they're ready to let them go
I wonder if they even know
I watch them falling
I watch the fall in

I'm just looking
Contemplating
What we're all in

I watch the boys down by the lake
Skimming stones, the best of mates
No thoughts are cast out for their fates
Just stones are cast, until water breaks

I look at the splash that's made
They drop not to be seen again
I watch them falling
I watch the fall in

I'm just looking
Contemplating
What we're all in

I watch the birds upon my lawn
None appear to be forlorn
They delight over the scattered seeds
I notice them, but they don't notice me

I look at the feathers they leave behind
That they scatter as they take to the sky
I watch them falling
I watch the fall in

I watch the second hand upon the clock
I know that it will never stop
Time disappearing, forever lost
The seconds that this watching cost

I wonder where the time has gone
And will we ever have it done
I watch them falling
I watch the fall in

Om

Here I am I grow
Learning what I know
Evolving to the soul
And on and on we go

I can feel it in my soul
I can feel it as I grow
I can take from you what you give me
That we already know
I can be part of the show
And create some more with flow

So just give me what I need
And the energy to see
I can take just what I need
And leave the rest of me so free
To create the energy
That evolves inside of me

And when you've given all you know
And relinquished it to flow
Then I can let you go
And you are free to flow
On to eternity
To the blissful energy
On to your loving song
Feel the energy that's Om

And then I will go
I can feel it in my soul
I have learnt all that you know
Now I creatively flow
Growing as I go
And giving as I leave
You will always be with me

And I can fully understand
The cycles of the land
The making of a world
That's inside me as a man
That's behind you as my god
As my teacher, as my lord
That's in front of me and stored
While I blissfully ignore

For ignorance is bliss
Until the understanding that I've missed
Brings me back to all we know
And connects us back to flow

And now we're great
It's our fate
We can blissfully create
The garden of our love
Sow our seeds and watch them grow
Watch them leave what they know
We will give them sight to see
They will take what they need

And we'll give back for what we took
In our action, in our books
In our paintings and our poetry
In the flowers and the trees
All the birds and the bees
All the land and the seas
In all that there will be
In our creativity

And once they have taken all they need
To grow to all that they will be
Then we're allowed to leave
And go to the energy
We have taken, we have learnt
We have firmly stood our ground

We have understood for now
Giving back for all we took
To the ending of our book

But we will love eternally
In the endless energy
That grows more blissfully
With each tide of the sea
Each in and out we breathe
To our soul journey that we're on
Inside the primordial Om

So it flows it carries on
You can live it through your song
You have given, passed it on
Long may this beauty carry on
And now they can let you go
They can give and let you flow
On and on to all that is
Through the dancing of the kids
On and on we grow
On and on we go

They will feel it in their soul
Eventually they'll let you go
On and on we carry on
To the rhythm of the Om

Happy Too

What do we know anyway?
What do we know?
What do we know any way?
What do we know?

We know we're going to die some day
What do we take when we go?
We may lose our mind some day
But we will never know

You don't take your possessions
You don't take your life's lessons
You don't take accolades or attributes
The things that are surrounding you

You don't take your eyes or your smile
You don't take your wife or your child
You don't take the way that you look
Or lessons unwittingly mistook

Maybe you take your mind
The deepness in you that you find
When you quieten your thoughts
And have a look down deep inside

You're consciousness
The blissfulness
That we hold inside of us
May be the only thing
That we take on with us
Bodies become dust
But that inner love
Maybe we take that
On to the after us

What do we know anyway?

As far as I know, land could be straight
You tell me that the earth is round
But it's not something I have found
You can say that smoking causes cancer
But I am not even a doctor
And even if I was
Can I see inside you?

Is there a god, or is there not?
How do you see it as a what?
Is there you, is there me?
Is it just imaginary?
I'm not being funny, but I've had a lucid dream
Is anything what it seems?
So why worry?
'Cause we don't even know

What a beautiful life show this is
Of which I'm a front row witness
And also I'm the lead role in
The stillness in each beginning
That continues with me breathing in

I know that happiness is a word
And some may feel this is absurd
But you can choose to be happy
In this moment just like me
It's perception don't you know?
Like where you are
And where you wan't to go

If you start with being thankful
For all the things you've got
And believe me there are people
That you'd rather you are not
And many people
That would rather they were you
So count your blessings friend
And you'll be happy too

Seeking

Spiritual process is a seeking
Religion is assuming things that you do not know
Spiritual exploration is what teaches
We don't know what we don't know we don't know

Now there's what we know for sure
And even some of that may not be true
And there's what's been found out before
But how much of that was found out by you

A Spiritual process is a seeking
Exploring inside is what you need to do
And that of the all around you
Every step you will learn more of the truth

Many religions have many good teachings
Practices to help you explore
But don't confine yourself to just one set
When there's so much more to adore

You do not have a duty
Towards anyone or anything
Keep love and care within your heart
You will always do the right thing
So keep on moving forward
And also keep on searching
You'll learn your way upon your path
And you'll keep on evolving

Agape

There exists the law of connection
When you transmit love and affection
When we all connect, it is meant to be
You'll rise up and come into agape

The Switches Of Happiness (Inspired By Deepak Chopra)

Give to your neighbour
Transmit love and light
Let go of things that do not best serve
Indulge in all you like
Give thanks for all that is
Forgive those that have hurt you
Give yourself and be of service
And happiness will find you

Eternity

Hold your head to the sky now, and breathe
Go ahead, close your eyes now, you'll see
There's much more inside of you
Than you thought there would be

The love that's within is greater
Than the love that's without
But those that won't risk it for love
Don't know what love's all about

So please, if it brings you peace
You may have the shoes from my feet
We both will have them at the end
And that's for eternity

I will give whatever I have
Because I know you are me
We are all part of the all
And that's for eternity

Take a minute to yourself now, and be
Still and quiet in your mind now, at peace
Take your awareness to your body
From your head to your feet

For in that moment of stillness
Soon I'm sure you will see
When your thoughts leave your mind
You're in eternity

A Woppa Bam A Loo Wop

A woppa bam a loo wop
A woppa bam a loo wop
You gotta have the cream if you're gonna have the rhubarb

A woppa bam a loo wop
A woppa bam a loo wop
You gotta break the ceiling if you're gonna have a new top

A wop doo up up a duppa do down
A wop doo up up a duppa do down
A dipping duppa doo up
We're up and not down
You better start the party
'Cause we're coming into town

We're going in
We're going up
A woppa bamma loo wop
A woppa bam boo
Yeah you better be ready
Or we'll go without you
Yeah

We're so electric and connected
We're downright source infected
Straight out on the stage
And we're gonna break a leg kid

We're rocking and popping
We're moving and grooving
We take a funky beat
And we put a little tune in
Lay down the funky lyrics
Are you ready baby, you in?

We're wop bamma a loo bop

We're woppa bam a looin

Doo dan up, we're boppa doppa doo dan
We doo dan up, a doppa doppa do dan
We blowing out the candles
Like I'm swinging round a fan
You gotta hit the sun waves
If you wanna catch a tan

A woppa bam a loo wop, a woppa bam bam

I'm picturing vast fields
A river running through it
Governments cooperating
Helping people through it
Sustainable living
Respecting what we're leaving
Everybody prospering
Sharing, kindness, giving

A woppa bam a loo wop
For everything that's living

A doo dup up, a duppa doo up
A doo dup up, a duppa doo up

Be thankful for the hand that's pulling you up
Thank you for the hand that's pulling us up

We're learning and we're teaching
As we're growing don't be preaching
But lead by example
As people being decent
Love one another
Your sisters and your brothers
Your fathers and your mothers

And we'll doo duppa wup up in a world full of love

Feel

I'm a crystal dream believer
Flow with the stream
One day I will leave her
She is the dream

Let go of my oars
And sail on to the sea

With each and every moment
Taking in what I see

And I feel
Feel my heart beating
Yes I feel
What I plant my seeds in

Going to feed the garden of my soul
Plant the seeds and let them grow

Nourish them with loving intent
Flourishing to all that is meant

Joy and bliss, gratitude and wellbeing
The sight to see what I should be seeing

And I feel
Feel my heart beating
Yes I feel
The grass I place my feet in

The endless fields of prosperity
That awaken the all that's inside of me

The Same

Don't only live for some future goal
Do miss the sides of the mountain
It's the slopes that sustain life
Not the peak covered in white

Though nothing is forever
And we should all accept change
We should stay connected to our hearts
Bring yourself back again

Beauty is all around us
It's the same for you and me
The beauty of a bird is the same for a child
As it is for the wise old lady

The scent of a flower
Has the same power
As the poor man on the street
Or the king up in the tower

Mad Max

His name is Mad Max
He's a catch
He's ready to snatch
Like a wolf pack

Oh oh

Ok so you think
Now you've had a drink
Out looking for love
And he looks enough

Oh oh

What are you looking for girl?
What are you looking for now?
What are you looking for girl?
What are you looking for?

As he two steps
Watch him take a sip
Of his bottled beer
Showing no fear

Oh oh

Shirt unbuttoned at the top
House music club
Looking quite rock
Torn jeans and some white socks

Oh oh

What are you looking for girl?
What are you looking for now?
What are you looking for girl?
What are you looking for?

His name is Mad Max
He's a catch
He's ready to snatch
Like a wolf pack

Oh oh

Oh oh

Oh yeah

Better think twice
Though he looks nice
One of those guys
With the dark eyes

He ain't gonna settle down girl
No no
He ain't gonna leave his world
No no

Oh oh
Oh oh

Oh yeah

What are you looking for girl?
What are you looking for now?
What are you looking for girl?
What are you looking for?

He'll take you home sure
And tell you that you're
Something that he's never seen before
But he'll leave tomorrow
Tomorrow
He'll leave

Oh oh

Oh oh

That's what you're looking for girl?

Cinderella

Cinderella
You're working yourself to the bone
Don't you know your future?
Darling don't you know?

Cinderella

Cinderella

I watch you sweeping
I watch you cleaning up after them
I watch you playing
With your imaginary friends

Cinderella

Oh Cinderella

Don't you know your future?
Don't you wish for more?

Cinderella

You're working yourself to the bone
Don't you know your future?
Darling don't you know?

Cinderella
Cinderella

I watch you lay down at night
Too tired to dream
I watch your silent desperation
Too afraid to scream

I feel your heartache
But yet I see you smile
The pain that you take
Cinderella

Working yourself to the bone
Cinderella

Take a look up to the stars
Watch one shoot past for you
Wish for your hopes and dreams
And know that they'll come true

Cinderella
Cinderella

I'm watching over you
I'm watching over you
I'm watching over you
All your wishes will come true

Up

We're going up
Up up up
Flying high
Celebrating life

Those tears that fall from your eyes
Through the river of life
Down to the sea
Then the sun shines
And you rise rise rise

And you rise
Feel it
Fly
You can fly

We're going up
Up up up
Flying high
Celebrating life

You can touch the sky

When knocked down
To the ground
Up you bounce
Turn around

We're going up
Once again now

Take you to the top

Nonstop
Like a rocket rock

See space and time
An expanding clock

Full of energy
Like an endless sea
Full of substances
Chemically
Take my hand
And come with me

Is it real?
Am I real?
Is your pineal
Pioneering this feel?
Inside of you
Like you're riding through
Multiple spheres
Another hemisphere
I'll remember here
My remaining years
Nothing's ever clear

Until the pop's stopping
Tops rocking
Rocks flopping
Socks popped off
Into stockings
Full of all the things
That the good deserve
From Father Wishmas
Full of dreams and wishes
Fun filled screams
And kisses
Finding kindness
In the blindness
This supernatural moment
That we're owning
All our own

Although we'd share it
With the world
If they'd bare it
They would swirl
To the love
That we all need
The energy

Upon which we feed
Like your favourite song
That picks you up
Up up up

We're going up
Up up up

Ascending
With no ending
Up

Happiness Comes From Your Heart

Happiness comes from your heart
Happiness comes from your heart
Happiness comes from your heart
Happiness comes from you heart

So why do we wait?
Why do we wait?
Why do we wait?
Why do we wait?

For the external to turn you
Into that which you seek from the inferno

Burn it all away
Burn it all away
Listen to you heart
Find another way

We should go inside
We should go inside
Not so we should hide
But to realise

Happiness comes from
Happiness comes from your heart
Happiness comes from
Happiness comes from your heart

Happiness comes

I can feel the love
I can feel the love
I can I can

I can feel the love

I can feel the love
I can I can

I can feel the love
I can feel the love
I can I can

Why do we wait?
Why do we wait?
And evaluate
As if it's our fate?

We can change our mind
We can stay and find
Love for what we got
Love for where we reside

Look at where we stand
We have come so far
And we understand
This is a choice of ours

Don't have to meditate
Or evaluate
You can change your fate
Change what's on your plate

Happiness is a state of mind
So let us change the state we find
Let us change it now it's time
Just say this very simple line

I'm happy yeah
Oh I'm happy
I'm happy yeah
Oh I'm happy

So is this all real?

Yes this is all real
Happiness I feel
With all it's appeal

Happiness comes from your heart
Happiness comes from your heart
Happiness comes from your heart
So join me now, let's start

What's On Your Mind

What's on your mind?
What's on your mind?
Won't you tell me?
What's on your mind?

And I'm not bothered about
What you've done before no no no

I just want to know
Where you want to go?
What's in front of you?
What's the current you?

Yeah Yeah

What's on your mind?

Whoa whoa whoa whoa
I just want to know
What is in your soul?
What is on your mind?

Never did I know what I know now
Forever in a moment in a somehow
A maybe sensibility
The whispers in the sanctuary

That holds me
Love embraces me
Endless possibilities

Lets go now

What's on your mind?
What's deep inside?

What might I find?
Let's celebrate life

What's on your mind?
What's on your mind?
Won't you tell me?
What's on your mind?

Up Until Now

I know some of you don't know this yet
And some know more than me
I just want to send this message
For those that are yet to see

My understanding up until now
The beauty of life that makes me proud
The sky that sits behind the cloud
The sound that sirens now allowed

We are all and all is love
The same thing is in all of us
We are all and all are one
Equally divine, everyone

Bring Yourself Into Bliss

Think of a child in laughter
Then cradling a baby in your arms
Notice how it makes you smile
Or brings a sense of calm

Think of seeing a loved one
And embracing them with a hug
Or a dog chasing a ball in the park
And flowers emerging from buds

Focus on a beautiful sunset
Or sunrise if you prefer
Notice what happens to your emotions
Watch as the happiness stirs

Think of a vast flowing meadow
Or a crystal clear blue sky
Focus on a teacher that's helped you
Or the apple of your eye

Focus on yourself in the mirror
With a wide grin upon your face
Think about childhood holidays
Adventure to your happy place

Remember a pet you are fond of
And hear the sweet sound of bird's song
Smell the scent of your favourite dish
Or a beautiful walk you went on

Focus on swimming in the ocean
If that is something you loved
A wonderful pool you once dived in
Or two elegant turtledoves

Focus on eating an ice cream
And as you try to catch the drips
Think about warm cake and custard
Or the softness of a kiss on your lips

Notice how it makes you feel
When you place your awareness in joy
You can bring yourself into bliss
Just by thinking of what you enjoy

In The Now

1 2 3 4
1 2 3 4

Here I am where I was before
In the now with a wish for more
I am here where I've always been
Past wisdom's felt inside of me
The future's not a time for now
There is no time when you're in the now

1234
1234

Breathe in, breathe out

Have a look at what's around
Smell and taste, hear the sounds
Feel physically and emotionally
Then give thanks, abundantly

Pick 5 things to be thankful for
In the now there are many more
Connect with your heart
It's from there you start
Now you're here, where else of course
You're now connected back to the source

1234
1234

You're in the now and that is perfect
A culmination of what's created
And with every now it's a fresh start
Re-imagine the desires of your heart

When you create them they will be set
In your future that's not seen yet
But soon you'll see that it's somehow
Gone from the future into your now
So be free, be thankful, enjoy and create
Have love and compassion in your heart
We love you, we're with you we're here in the now
We're the love and compassion in your heart

1234
1234

We're here again
Where we were before

In the now
Where we'll always be
In the now
Where we'll always be

Connect With Your Heart

How do you connect with your heart?
How do I reflect, where do I start?
It all starts with self love
Feed yourself first to first be enough

When the oxygen mask drops down
You first have to put it on your own mouth
Steady yourself so you can breath
You can help your children once you're free
Then you can help those close to you
When you've helped them they can all help too
Until everyone that can be reached
Can now be reached
And now they breath
Freely flowing from their hearts

Follow your aliveness
And see where it will guide you
Connected with alignment
Centred in your heart

You will have plenty of choices
You're guided by your divine spirit
You can always feel the right choice
You can feel it, you are near it
Intuition is your best friend
It allows you to choose
When you should be standing strong
And when you should be loose

You will find your life's purpose
If you detach from your thought
Allow yourself to surface
Where you were before
Connected purely with your heart

Ask it where to make a start
Purpose will then find you
It is something that you are

Follow your aliveness
And see where it will guide us
Connected with alignment
Centred in your heart

Wonderful lessons you will learn
And wonderful wisdom you'll pass on
Listen to your intuition
Make your choices on your mission
If you can act with vigour, you will have the will
Some will find it's found, when they're just sitting still
How do you connect with yours?
Yoga, painting, riding horses?
Singing, writing, piano?
Feel excitement, then you'll know
Do the things where you feel love
Know that it's more than enough
It allows you to contact your heart
And the ripple effect will then start
Heart by heart we change the world
One at a time in an upwards whirl
Feel the love and feel alive
Connect to source and then you thrive
Then affect another's life
Then many lives, we're all alive
Consciousness grows and expands
No more needy, empty hands
Just pure hearts, strong and in love
Then we all can rise above
And when our consciousness has risen
We can all ascend to our perfect heavens

So let's
Follow our aliveness

And see where it will guide us
Connected with alignment
Centred in our hearts

Expanding on so far
Expanding from our hearts

Rap Love

Hello I'm here, get used to me
Spread this message, positivity
And it all comes flowing naturally
Like a flow that you know is meant to be

Through the years the rap game is
All about pain is
The struggle, the strain it's
Trouble drug game it's

About time we talk about
What we want
Not what we don't
And you'll see it won't

Come into our reality
No negative productivity
Just the positive, positively

The knowledge has come here finally

Please fine tune me
What it needs to be
Focus on what you want and you will see

Don't tell me about the hate and the crime
The pain and the struggle, the hateful times
You can rap positive and make it rhyme
Keep the flow, here we go, find your next line

So listen to me, let's change the game
Change the way you look at things
And look, they change

So come with me and do the same

Change the way you look at things
Watch them change

Think of all that you want to be
And focus on the vision clearly
Make sure it's one that you want to see
Spit it out lay it down, reality

Oh you want people to understand
About the way of life that is underground
About the hard times you need to withstand
But those ripples will spread out across the land

Really more than that sole objective
Find a better way for a soul to let live
You strive and try for your life above
You got to change your focus to that of love

Give what you can and never steal
Be real to yourself and what you feel
You know that love is, what feels right
Choose life and love and it'll be alright

It'll be alright
It'll be alright

Trust me, I can see, what's above me
And all that's gonna be in front of me
This message is love spiritually
It's not physically or mentally

All that there is
Adults or kids
You can all do this
It's not a myth

I know it's true
Listen what to do
And all of you

Can do it too

Hold it in your head
Believe it's true
And what I feel
You'll feel it too

What I feel, you'll feel it too

I want to see
All those little seeds
Grow through the concrete
To all that they can be
So listen to me
Spit positivity
What you're focusing on
Will be reality

You'll find your mind has been lying
It may not be working, even though you're trying
If you follow your heart
It'll set you apart

Now that you've started
No dearly departed
Screw it up and park it
Let go of the darkness

Follow me to the light
You'll see it feels right
Then finally
You will be
Anything that you want to be
Go where you want
See what you want to see

Then life will go on and you will come up
You already have love, just never give up

Just Want You To Know

I just want you to know
I just want you to know
That there's
Nowhere we can't go
Nowhere we can't go

I'll be holding onto you
When you're holding onton me
And we'll find our route
To serenity

I just want you to know
I just want you to know
That there's
Nowhere we can't go
Nowhere we can't go

I'll be giving it to you
When you're giving it to me
And we'll be finding a route
To serenity

So hold on
Close to me now
Just hold on
So close to me now

'Cause no matter the odds
And no matter the trials
We will overcome all
And be free and wild

I just want you to know
I just want you to know
That there's

Nowhere we can't go
Nowhere we can't go

Over the top and to the end of time
Through times forgotten
And times flying by

You'll be mine
And I'll be by your side
No concept of time
And nowhere we can't hide

I know that you know
Oh, I know that you know
That there's
Nowhere that we can't go

I know that you know
Oh I know that you know
That there's
Nowhere that we can't go

Taking My Time

I've been taking my time
Just to realise
The scent of fine wines
And open fires
Just to get back to you
And the way were
Before all of the time
Seemed to take its turns

Oh I've been taking the time
Just to realise
The scent of fine wines
And open fires
Just to get back to you
And the way were
Before all of the time
Seemed to take its turns

And maybe we'll find
A new place for us
Below the night sky
And all the stars

A place we can be
What we used to be
Where I'm all for you
And you're all for me

And maybe it's time
That we take the time
To realise
When to get in line
Just to get back to you
And the way we were
Before all of the time

Seemed to take its turns

'Cause baby there is only you
Only you in my heart
Baby there is only you
And for you I would do anything that I need to do
Just for you to see me and for me to see right back to you

And I say anything and everything
Everything there's ever been
Is just time culminating
Over what we should do

The Come Down

Hold on now
What's that there
I try to stay strong
I thought I was there

But this has got me
And I don't think it should
My thinking's no good
Where has the zen gone
Why can't I quieten my mind
Where is the stillness that I always could find
What's made this engulf me and leave that behind
Leave that behind

Let me be strong
Let me feel love
Let me wash this away
And live to cry another day

I know I am strength
I know I am power
So in this weakest hour
Please bring me the faith

I know I can push through
I'll give my love to you
I'll sing hallelujah
As that brings me to ya
To the understanding that gives understanding
The passion of compassion
The love of the love

Let it wash over me
And bring me strength from above
I can die and lose the love

To be reborn again

Stronger
Wiser

Let me be strong
Let me feel love
Let me wash this away
And live to cry another day

To love the shade and appreciate it's pain
To be reborn to the light again
And appreciate that

To stay connected in greater depth
In the now that we've come to
I know that it will bring to me
The blissful destruction
And serenity
The pain that is necessary
To know the contrast in ecstasy

So don't lose faith in what I am
I'm only man
An all that man is
The wisdom, strength and power
That washes away with the final shower
That brings us back to pureness
At source
And allows us to follow the given course
To realise infallibility
And that which brings me back to me

So thank you darkness
Thank you shade
Your contrast I always forgave
To lead me on to brighter days
And intensity of the source's rays

Let me be strong
Let me feel love
Let me wash this away
And live to cry another day

Thank you pain and thank you sorrow
For guiding me to my tomorrow

I'm always love
And that I trust
I continue to flow
And that's enough

Fran's Song

I was taught that you're amazing
But then told my crazy
Is something to conceal?
Hide away, think how others feel?
Well that's not real

Everybody has their own gift
Everyone should find out what it is
It's what brings you bliss
Deep down inside
You know it feels right

When I let my singing go
It was like leaving my soul
And I went missing
I'm always signing
I'm always singing
Deep inside of me

I stopped listening to music
It was too hard for me
Painfully ashamed
Of what I'm meant to be

But I say no

I want to hear the beauty beauty
I want to feel the beauty beauty
I want to be the beauty beauty
I know I am beautiful

I won't let you do it to me no no
I won't let you do it to me no no

I was told to grow up
And get a proper job
Told to be an adult
But what's a proper job?

I'm a singer, that's what's inside of me
Please let this song bird fly and be free
And actually what you will see

What I am is glorious, so let me be

Then it can grow and bloom
And be wild like a flower
Growing curiously, to my finest hour
Open to the elements
And realise my power

I want to hear the beauty beauty
I want to feel the beauty beauty
I want to be the beauty beauty
I know I am beautiful

Don't fear your own beauty no no
Don't fear your own beauty no no

It's only through the process
That you will flourish
Then shine and be bright
Give back and nourish

Give beauty to the world
Like the clam that gives the pearl
And then inspire others
As our fathers and our mothers

We know what we're here for
We know why we're here
To sing our songs of life
For all to hear

We want to hear the beauty beauty
We want to feel the beauty beauty
We want to be the beauty beauty
We know we are beautiful

Nothing But Good Vibes

It's the shift that brings us
Off the path of fear
To the path of light,
Towards the light that's near
You may feel safe
In your comfy fear
Because you know what it is,
But don't know what is near

And furthermore
You can't leave your thirst
What's there to endure?
Soon that bubble bursts

You know that you have to relinquish it
And go into the unknown
To get your abundance
Your rightful flow
That's what faith is
Faith is to go
Walk open eyed straight into
What you're yet to know is even true
But to realise and prove
All you felt through you
And that's what's real
All you feel
Live your song
Sing your life
Be free
Flourish
Shine
And thrive

Nothing but good vibes coming from me
Nothing but good vibes coming from me

And if you listen on I'm sure you'll see
There's nothing but good vibes coming from me

Anything is possible
As long as you believe
Set your mind to it
And I'm sure you will achieve
Listen to the message that I'm telling you today
Act and belief and there'll always be a way

No matter what you want
You can go and get it
Put it in your mind
And then you set it
Move towards it with every moment you can
Take the best action to orchestrate your plan

Now don't get confused
With what you gotta do
If you haven't got a plan yet
It'll come to you
Just know what you want
And be positive
Go out into the world
With that as the way you live
Quieten your mind
When you cannot find
Something directly linked
To your purpose line
Trust me on this
The path will come clear
And every moment of life
You'll be getting nearer

Nothing but good vibes coming from me
Nothing but good vibes coming from me
And if you listen on I'm sure you'll see
There's nothing but good vibes coming from me

If you feel the urge then stomp your feet
And always converse with the people you meet
Keep your eyes wide open for synchronicity
And watch how easily your dream becomes reality

Oh just follow your urges
Yeah just follow your urges
Those instincts
Those instincts
Are sent to urge us

Golden Child

We are all children with golden hearts
We are all golden at our start
Time may test you
You feel you're less special
Or less golden
Please hang on, hold on

Who we were when we were children
Is who we are always meant to be

We then go down a different path
Training not to be what we are
It doesn't matter just how far
We'll always come back to where we are
It hits us and then we smile
The purity of our inner child
Why don't we just play here a while
And sit within our golden child

We are all still children
We will always be children
We are all still children
Golden children

I used to believe
That I could do anything
I could be anything
Be anything

As I got older
With the world on my shoulders
Stuck between a hard place
And a very large boulder

Forcing me and squeezing me
Why submission? Why retreat?

Please see through your child eyes
The world is always at your feet

I used to believe that I could fly so high
Touch the limits of the beautiful great blue sky

I would put my coat on the wrong way round
This cape that I made helps me save a town

Feel all the feelings and hear the sounds
Chew it up and see what my mind spits out

It was always beautiful and always so pure
Boundless energy flowing from my inner core

We are all still children
We will always be children
We are all still children
Golden children

Even though we've sinned and made all of our mistakes
We always have time to repair what we may break
We are all still dreaming, little dreaming babies
Learning through the waves, and the waving daisies
I can centre back to what's inside of me
And always find the true inner child in me

The true element of purity
I was gifted and kind
I was pure and free

Full of hope
And so much more
Always with a focus
On something I adore

We are all still children
We will always be children
We are all still children

Golden children

Have I changed?
Have I changed?

Nope

That's me, I'm him
I'm the child within
And I'm always here
A new beginning
Still as special as I always was
Why could you lose something just because?
I may have lost the innocence
But I still have the inner strength

The sense of soul
The belief of goals
The heart of a star
The leading role

Achieved before they were even believed
I can never lose what's inside of me
Physically you can make me bleed
But my inner child will never leave

We are all pureness at the start
So if we learn to follow our hearts
We'll be our youthful purity forever
You'll find that you can come back to me whenever

I know I may have left and I might leave again
But I'll always come back my imaginary friend
I know that this time I've been gone a while
But now I'm back, new beginning
Golden child

Imagination (House Track)

A true sign of intelligence is
Imagination
Imagination

There's no need to reminisce
Imagination
Imagination

I feel it in my soul
It's coming from my soul
It drives me to my goal
I feel it head to toe

It takes me on to my true fire
It symbolises my desire

Imagination
Imagination

Imagination is more important than knowledge

All this intelligence
I don't need it in my life
I don't need it in my life
What I am feeling is right

Imagination
Imagination

Knowledge may define everything that we know
But imagination will show us where we should go

Knowledge may define everything that we know
But imagination will show us where we should go

Where we need to go
Where we need to go
Where we need to go

Where we need to
We need to
We need to
We need to
We need to
We need to
We need to go

So use your imagination
So use your imagination
So use your imagination
So use your imagination

It points to
It points to
It points to
It points to

All we might yet discover
All we might yet create
All we might yet discover
All we might yet create
All we might yet discover
All we might yet create
All we might yet discover
All we might yet create

All we might
All we might
All we might
All we might
All we might
All we might
All we might

All we might
All we might
All we might
All we might
Yet create

Imagination
Imagination
Imagination

So please will you use your imagination

Knowledge may define everything that we know
But imagination will show us where we should go

Knowledge may define everything that we know
But imagination will show us where we should go

Where we need to go
Where we need to go
Where we need to go
Where we need to go

All we might yet discover
All we might yet create
All we might yet discover
All we might yet create
All we might yet discover
All we might yet create
All we might yet discover
All we might yet create

Imagination is the guide, to take on us on to our fate

Our fate
Our fate
Our fate

Love What You Got

If you listen to a woman's intuition
She will lead you to a lake
Where the moonlight glistens
She will take you on the swings
And teach you how to fly
And it may be raining
But that just adds to the sky

You got to love what you got and what you love will come
Love where you're at and your love will come back
You got to love what you got and what you love will come
Love where you're at and your love will come back

So you can dance along
And sing this song
And all you need
Will soon come along
Just thank where you are
And thank what you got
'Cause no matter who you are
You have got a lot

We've all got the power
Of the beautiful sunflower
To brighten up our world
Because remember it is ours
The earth is the mother
That provides it all for you
And the sun is the father
That will always guide you through

You got to love what you got and what you love will come
Love where you're at and your love will come back
You got to love what you got and what you love will come
Love where you're at and your love will come back

So stroll through the magic forest
And feel the love from the trees
Breathe in deeply
On the cool country breeze
Dance in the sunshine

And you will never freeze
Think of what you want
And what you want will be

So no matter where you're at
Embrace what you got
And all that you love
Will soon be a lot
You just have to have faith
And believe it will be
To joyously create
In this land of the free

You got to love what you got and what you love will come
Love where you're at and your love will come back
You got to love what you got and what you love will come
Love where you're at and your love will come back

And if you listen
To your own intuition
It will guide you to a well
Where there will be the children
And in that deep deep well
They can all make all their wishes
And they will all come true
As long as we believe it

Love what you got
And what you love will come
Now you see
That our love has begun

As consciousness expands
You soon will see
Love is bliss
So love blissfully

Dearly Departed

I feel it starts where we come from
And from there we always carry on
And I know we'll all meet at the end
And foes will always end up friends

Pureness
At start
Pure souls
Pure hearts

Never in question
Dearly departed
Take us back to
Where we started

I want you to
Feel my love
I want you to
Know that you are enough

I want you to
Know that it's OK
I want you to
Go on your own way

I feel it starts where we come from
And from there we always carry on
And I know we'll all meet at the end
And foes will always end up friends

Pureness
At start
Pure souls
Pure hearts

Never in question
Dearly departed
Take us back to
Where we started

I want you to

Feel your worth
I want you to
Find peace on Earth

I want you to
Find your purpose
I want you to
Know that you deserve it

I feel it starts
It starts where we come from
And from there from there from there
We will always carry on

We will always carry on
We will always carry on
And we will all meet at the end
And our foes will be friends

Pureness
At start
Pure souls
Pure hearts

Pureness
At start
Pure souls
Pure hearts

Oh I want you, I want you, I want you to
I want you, I want you, I want you to
Feel it, yes feel it inside of you
Feel it, yes feel it inside of you

Feel it inside of you

Dearly departed
When we're back where we started
You'll be there too

Go Forth

Go forth
With love and care in your heart
And you'll already be there
You don't need to start

You don't need to change
Change will come to you
You don't need to question
Your path will be true

Go forth
With love and care in your heart
And you'll be doing all you should
Wherever you are

You don't need to chase it
You're already there
When your heart is filled
With love and care

A Hippy At Heart

I'm a hippy at heart
But what is a hippy?
I go through life
So that it reminds me

I come from love
Always from love
I feel like sometimes
We think we're above

That which we are
That may not be far
And at other times
We're as far as the stars

So have fun and games
Enjoy your life
Remember that you are connected
 And that you thrive

And when we lay everything
Out on the bed
Because why not
Let's do that instead
Life may just start
To become much clearer
In the direction
That's leading us here

Because we are all on
A journey of life
We all get to see
The emotions of life

And we come through
Life as we do

Beginning to see
Versions of truth

So have fun and games
Enjoy your life
Remember that you are connected
And that you thrive

Even know you think you know
What's going on in your mind
The world can still sometimes be
A big thing outside of your mind

And that's OK
That's OK
That's OK

It may be a jungle out there
But there's no need to be scared
Adventure forward and you'll know
That you are already prepared

So wander where your lust will take you
And your love will bring you back to you
Like every vision that creation winds
Coming together, all at the same time

And thats OK
That's OK
That's OK

So have fun and games
Enjoy your life
Remember that you are connected

And that you thrive
And that you thrive

Come Out Of Myself

Lying in bed with a heavy head
Can't think what to do
My girls gone left me, the anger's gone
Can't decide if I'm feeling blue
Is this just a phase, I realise my gaze
Staring at space in my room
Is it time at last for us to part paths?
Or just something we must work through?

You'll always be my one girl
But always questioning if I am yours
You'll always be my sun girl
But can't feel your rays while I'm indoors
Just need to come out of myself
And realise I'm good enough
Just need to be myself
And start to feel my love

I know that whatever happens to us
The right path will prevail
Sometimes the ship don't seem strong enough
But onwards it will sail
You said that your gone for good this time
But I don't know what to believe
The thought of being without you
Isn't something I conceive

As I lie here baby, am I going crazy
In my head for you?
Felt you put your family before my child
That made us argue
You got your back up girl, and said some shit
That you know just ain't true
I did the same and and went inside my brain
Pulled out some pain for you

You'll always be my one girl
But always questioning if I am yours
You'll always be my sun girl
But can't feel your rays while I'm indoors
Just need to come out of myself
And realise I'm good enough
Just need to be myself
And start to feel my love

I was good before, but when we met
I just felt complete
So when truth be told, you filled the hole
That was inside of me
Know we have our issues, the time we mis-use
Used ungratefully
But I know we'll work through, I know we'll get to
Our own heavenly

Tell me what I can say, how to change this day
From darkness into light
How do we get away, from what we know is wrong
And back to what is right?

I will swallow my pride for you, apologise to you
I will hold you tight
I will happily run to you, lie down and comfort you
And say you're always right

You'll always be my one girl
But always questioning if I am yours
You'll always be my sun girl
But can't feel your rays while I'm indoors
Just need to come out of myself
And realise I'm good enough
Just need to be myself
And start to feel my love

I'm sorry my baby, I know I was crazy
For what it is worth
Sorry for what I said and how I treated you
That you didn't deserve
You are my girl baby, whole wide world baby
My heavens and my earth
I hate I've done you wrong, but I love you more
Than I can put into words

So I'm lying in bed, still with a heavy head
Tell me what to do
Wiping away the tears that I have shed
Know that I'm feeling blue
Please be just a phase, I can't face the days
If they are without you
It's not time for us to part paths
This is something we'll work through

You'll always be my one girl
No longer questioning if I am yours
You'll always be my sun girl
But can't feel your rays while I'm indoors
So now I've come out of myself
And realised I'm good enough
I'm always going to be myself
And start to feel your love

We just need to be ourselves and we'll stay here in love

Be The Change

We all have a choice
As a united consciousness
The love of power
Or the power of love

Today you can decide
To act with love
Or to ignore that which
Is already upon us
We all have a decision point
This could be yours
Stay chasing power
Or have love as your cause

We all have our decision points
What will you do with yours?
Understand your world?
Align your purpose?
Be the change?

Or go back to your screen
And eat burgers again
Throw your plastic in the trash
And drive old petrol cars
The least resistance for now
Won't get you that far

Put in some effort
Know how to help
Be the change
Evolve for the world

Become the healing
Become the cooperation
Become the peace

Live that and love that

The change must start within ourselves
Before it can start across the world
What is it that you see in yourself?
That you don't like about your world
If you can be honest and change those things
Then the world will follow, and your heart will sing

I change the world
As I see it
Identify the change
And then be it

Morning Mantra Song

Sing this song with me in the morning
And let it guide your soul through the day
Trust that what you sing will guide you well
The mantra that your heart wants you to say

So close your eyes and follow your breath
And sing these words with me
You'll notice your breath slows down
By itself naturally

And sing

Joyful energetic body
Loving compassionate heart
Reflective alert mind
Lightness of being

Joyful energetic body
Loving compassionate heart
Reflective alert mind
Lightness of being

May the highest good be done for all
May the highest good be done for all

May the divine
Flow through me
May the divine
Flow through me
Joyful energetic body
Loving compassionate heart
Reflective alert mind
Lightness of being

Joyful energetic body

Loving compassionate heart
Reflective alert mind
Lightness of being

This message is sent with love
For one and for all
With love and care in our hearts
The highest good will be done for all

Biggest Fan

Thank you, thank you
Thank you, thank you
Thank you, thank you
Thank you, thank you

Thank you for supporting me
Thank you for what it is you see
Thank you for the love you show
Thank you for helping me grow

Thank you, thank you
Thank you, thank you
Thank you, thank you
Thank you, thank you

Thank you for your kind words
Thank you for what it is you heard
Thank you for coming out tonight
Thank you for saying it sounds alright

Thank you for all of your applause
Thank you for opening all the doors
Thank you for that continued support
Thank you for all those happy thoughts

Thank you, thank you
Thank you, thank you
Thank you, thank you
Thank you, thank you

Thank you for all your kind reviews
Thank you for listening to my views
Thank you for all that you have been
Thank you for continuing to be

Thank you for listening to the words
Thank you for sending them onwards
Thank you for taking it all in
Thanks for being there from the beginning

Thank you, thank you
I love you, love you
Thank you, thank you
I love you, love you
Thank you, thank you
I really do love you

Thank you for all of your belief
Thank you for all you've given me
Thank you for how much you understand
Thank you so much, I'm your biggest fan

Listen To Your Heart

If something doesn't feel right
Then stop it right away

You may feel that there's no other way
But if you trust yourself your heart will say:

Trust in me my love
And I will guide you true
Have faith in me my child
And let me guide you through

To love and light
And beyond
To do what's right
And carry on

How To Help?

I'm not so arrogant as to think I know what is
The best thing for everyone to reach eternal bliss
So I will carry on through life going with the flow
With care and love in my heart and with these I will know

That I am contributing
The best way that I can
To the highest good for all
Giving to the plan

I had grand illusions
Of what I could do to help
Saving those that probably
Think that we need help

But now I know the way to go
Live each day within the flow
And watch the wonders as we go
With care and love within our soul

What Is Our Reason?

I don't really know how we all got here
I just want to know where we're all going
I don't really know how we found ourselves together
I just want to know we'll be together at the end

I don't ever ask where our love came from
I don't need to ask that our love will last forever
I already know our love's without condition
I just want to know our life's endeavour

Because we came here for a reason
And that I know for sure
What is our reason for living?
We thrive, explore and adore

What Are We?

So here we are
What are we?
Evolution
Spirituality
The endless striving to develop
Beings thriving through the ever
So I'll try to be true forever
And teach and learn as I go

Man was made with a wayward spirit
The element of irreducible rascality
Just a pinch of which is in us all
Our inner child is adding to our fantasies

Do you have the patience to wait until the mud settles and the water is
clear?
Do you have the courage to tell your own truth and let people know why
you're here?

So here we are
What are we?
Evolution
Spirituality
The endless striving to develop
Beings thriving through the ever
So I'll try to be true forever
And teach and learn as I go

You think you know what you want
The big house, big car and the status
But open your eyes to the propaganda
All we want is in fact inside us

I have chased it, I have had it
Earned the most I can, usually to give it

Life is here so we can live it
Love it, learn it, hold it, trust it

So here we are
What are we?
Evolution
Spirituality
The endless striving to develop
Beings thriving through the ever
So I'll try to be true forever
And teach and learn as I go

Awakening is about letting go
Give it all away and then you'll know
That what you need was there all along
The love in your heart and the voice for your song

The connection to all and the feeling of being
The beauty of the world and the vision to see it
The dancing soul and the music you're hearing
The vast universe and the wisdom to be it

So here we are
What are we?
Evolution
Spirituality
The endless striving to develop
Beings thriving through the ever
So I'll try to be true forever
And teach and learn as I go

For time is endless and we have it all
So soon we'll graduate from life's school
The teacher will become the master
And we'll live happily ever after

We'll be love, love will be us
And that's enough for all of us

Eternity in our nirvana
No longer child, we'll be the father

So there we are
We are love
Evolved to all
All of us

Great Grand Mother Load

Give me the great grand mother load
Give me that cheat code
To the life that we know
The great grand mother load

Give me the strength within
A voice for me to sing
Give me the vision that I need
To see all that I wish to see

Take me to the stars
And show me flying cars
I wish to travel on the wind
I wish to find the light within

Give me the great grand mother load
Give me that cheat code
To the life that we know
The great grand mother load

Show me the faces of the places
That only few have seen
Allow me to fly high
In the solace of my dreams

Let me swirl in the whirlwinds
Go back to where time begins
Eradicate all my sins
I wish to find the light within

Let me climb to the mountaintop
And then don't stop
Stairway up to heaven
To find the holy gates unlocked

Give me the great grand mother load
Give me that cheat code
To the life that we know
The great grand mother load

I want to have it all
And give it all away
Live for a million days
In every single way

I want the multitude
Of golden avenues
Beyond the drugs and booze
Within which I can lose

I want the master plan
The maps of all the lands
The best of helping hands
Everything that's known to man

I want that great grand mother load
That secret cheat code
That as soon as I know
Will allow me to go

You Do You And I'll Do Me

So our stories start both London South East
I didn't know you and you didn't know me
Collecting different pieces to half of a puzzle
Having different highs and having different struggles

Music in our hearts and rhythm in our feet
Learning different crafts in the London streets
Oblivious to the fact that one day we'd meet
To create little pieces of history

And your best friend was my best friend, now we're best friends
Plenty of starts, plenty of middles and plenty of ends
The ups and downs and rounds and rounds
The smiles and laughs, cities and towns
Two years went by, side by side, the best of times

So you do you, and I'll do me
Each following our hearts
How it should be
Make sure you stop in life regularly
To look around and see
What's meant to be

I knew that I knew you but I didn't know ya
Both arms in the air on life's roller coaster
Rolling along obliviously
You do you and I'll do me

Seeing all of the sights and all of the places
But never taking in what was in front of our faces

I went to Liverpool to follow my heart
We felt the distance of being apart
Rolling along obliviously
You doing you and me doing me

I lived in love with the love of my life
At the same time you found yours
Still spoke enough and caught up now and then
Never knowing we were meant for more

And your best friend was my best friend, now we're best friends
Plenty of starts, plenty of middles and plenty of ends
The ups and downs and rounds and rounds
The smiles and laughs, cities and towns
Two years went by, side by side, the best of times

So you do you, and I'll do me
Each following our hearts
How it's meant to be
Make sure you stop in life regularly
To look around and see
What's meant to be

And it wasn't until a couple of weeks later
Having normal fun being what normal mates are
You happened to pick up a mate's old guitar
I sang some lyrics though not much of a singer

Like a bolt of lighting that hit us both
You gotta be kidding, this must be a joke
Exactly what we had both longed to find
Was in front of our faces this whole bloody time

Both longing to create musically
All I needed was you, all you needed was me
Now we both create most succinctly
You doing you and me doing me

But now we see
The connectivity
I'm doing you
And you're doing me

All You Want

First of all, you have to do you
It's the most unselfish thing to do
Being selfish first is the key
To do what's best for humanity

Once you've filled up your cup
And spill over the edges
The flow can go out to inspire
The ripples with no edges

Know what you want, write it down
Read it daily nice and loud
Focus on it then go out
Listen clearly and look out

You will find that all you need
Will be falling at your feet
Act upon the opportunities
And your dreams become reality

Milk every moment for all you can
Create the future without a plan
All that you need to endure
Will bring you to what you adore

Have faith that life will take you there
Know what you want and be aware
Life will present you with the omens
That will direct you to where you're going

Try to increase what you believe
And evolution will achieve
All that is and all that will be
The perfect synchronicity

So put a smile on your face
And be thankful that you've reached this place
Every moment is a gift
Well done for receiving this

Go forth now with bliss and joy
You are the writer of your story
Visualise all that you want
And appreciate all that you've got

All you need is to believe
And all you want soon will be

Freedom

Endure your turmoils with a smile
Where you are is always where you're meant to be
They will take you on to a better future
A future where you are free

We are not human beings
Immersed in a spiritual experience
We are in fact spiritual beings
Immersed in a human experience

Breathe in the essence and blow out the pain
Breathe in the love and blow out the strain
Feel your way
Live by your aura

It will guide you to freedom

Freedom, freedom

Clear your mind
And you will find
What is understood by the sunshine
What is loved by nature and the divine
Freedom, freedom

Love is you
And you are love
The ground beneath
The sky above

The universe is connected to you
And if you connect you will feel it too

Freedom, freedom

Say thank you for the all that is
Thank you for all that is
Thank you for eternal bliss
And freedom, freedom

Guide me to where I need to be
Show me the way
Allow me to see
Guide me to where I need to be
I thank you for showing me the way

Endure and adore each other
You are all part of the same
Forgive all and you will find
Freedom, freedom

Lockdown

I'm sitting inside
I can't go outside
Will I lose my mind?
No sense of time
There's no space to unwind
No friends by my side
Nowhere to go
Much more to know
If I go inside

You feel all alone
Trapped in your home
The people you're with
They get too well known

No more questions to ask
No more games you can play
No more songs you can sing
No more words you can say

But hold on
Can I hold my song?
Can I hold my words?
And still carry on?

When I can only walk
Around my block
Maybe I should sit still
And study my thoughts
Do I look to the future?
And things I think I should do
Or do I look to the past?
All the things that I've been through

Do I make believe

Some scenes false and some true
I study my thoughts
But with nothing for me to do

Nothing to judge
No need for a point of view
I just become the observer
And find myself in what's true

There is no need to panic
There is no need to rush
You can sit and observe
And that is enough

To observe and not judge
The highest intelligence
The highest of intellect
The highest of sense

All will be well
And all will be right
When you're gifted my darling
With the observer's sight

Be Blissful, Be Happy

Here's a little song I love
With a few little changes for all of us
Be blissful
Be happy

Every day you'll see some bliss
If you look you can be sure of this
Be blissful
Be happy

Oooo oo oo oo oo oo oo ooooo

If there's something that makes you smile
Shine awareness on it and wait a while

Be blissful be happy

Oooo oo oo oo oo oo oo ooooo

Every day when we first wake up
Let us first contemplate how great things are
Be blissful
Be happy

Everyone, no matter who you are
Can be nurtured by the earth
Or look upon a star
Be blissful
Be happy

'Cause when you smile and look around
There's another smile that can be found
Be blissful
Be happy

Oooo oo oo oo oo oo oo ooooo

A Heart That Yearns

The pink whispers of clouds on a sunset sky
The coolness of evening wind on the skin
The rustle of the leaves on a nearby tree
The sense of stillness in the movement

The depth of consideration
The timelessness of clarity
The deprivation of addiction
The start of something beautiful

A heart that yearns
A provoked thought
The hum of silence
The stillness

A stirring
A murmur
Love
In flow

That Beautiful Sunshine

Wake up in the morning
I am yawning
Feeling good

Wake up in the morning
I am yawning
Feeling good

Stretch out
Through my body
Getting limber
Feeling good

Sipping on my coffee
With a smile
I'm feeling good

Open up the curtains
And I give thanks for the day

I can feel the heat of the sun shining on me

That beautiful sunshine
That beautiful sunshine
Beautiful sunshine
That beautiful sunshine

Sun shine on me
Oh sun shine on me
Sun shine on me
Oh sun shine on me

Start to move my body
Move my feet
I'm feeling good

Got that dancing feeling
As I move
I'm feeling good

I step out of my door
And I give thanks for the day

I can feel the heat of the sun shining on me

That beautiful sunshine
That beautiful sunshine
Beautiful sunshine
That beautiful sunshine

Sun shine on me
Oh sun shine on me
Sun shine on me
Oh sun shine on me

Thank you for the sunshine
Thank you for the love
Thank you for the rays of light
That shine on all of us

That beautiful sunshine
That beautiful sunshine
Beautiful sunshine
That beautiful sunshine

Sun shine on me
Oh sun shine on me
Sun shine on me
Sun shine on me

Sugar

Give me some sugar sugar
Give me some cream
I can stir it in baby
Stir it with me

Give me some sugar sugar
And I'll give you your dreams
I will make them happen baby
Come and live them with me

Live them with me

We can take a sailboat
and sail on sail on
In abundance will we float
And I'll sing you my songs

There is no horizon
That we can not cross

Just give me that sugar baby
And make it sweet for us

Give me some sugar sugar
Give me some cream
I can stir it in baby
Stir it with me

Give me some sugar sugar
And I'll give you your dreams
I will make them happen baby
Come and live them with me

Live them with me

We can take a jet baby
And fly on fly on
In abundance we will soar
And I'll sing you my songs

There is no flight path
That we cannot take

Just give me that sugar baby
So we make that cake

Sugar
You are my sweet sensation
Sugar
My emancipation
Sugar, sugar, sugar
Sugar, sugar, sugar
Yeah

Give me some sugar sugar
Give me some cream
I can stir it in baby
Stir it with me

Give me some sugar sugar
And I'll give you your dreams
I will make them happen baby
Come and live them with me

Live them with me

Through The Forest

I'll take you through the forest
You'll take me by the hand
I'll take you on the forest floor
And make you understand

I'll show to you my darling
What you've never felt before
As we embrace my angel
Upon the forest floor

Where our road will take us
Does not need to be seen
Our love will stand strong
We are forever green

I'll dance with you in parking lots
And jump in muddy puddles
I'll blow you midnight kisses
And smother you in cuddles

I'll take you through the forest
You'll take me by the hand
I'll take you on the forest floor
And make you understand

Forever young my darling
You are within my eyes
Sunset boulevards and mountain climbs
We'll drink expensive wines

From night clubs
To beach parties
Art hubs and libraries
From horseback riding
Across wandering hills

To abandoned caves
And quiet windmills

I'll sit with you in hot springs
And we'll dive in deepest oceans
We'll lay on white sand beaches
And I'll rub you down with lotion

I'll take you through the forest
You'll take me by the hand
I'll take you on the forest floor
And make you understand

We will wander through our love my love
Wherever we will go
It really matters not my love
Because you'll already know

Your Light

Light
I'm just looking for that light
The one that helps shine on me
And give me clarity

The one that illuminates me
All of me

We all have our perfect purpose
And we all have our part to play
We can touch the ground and let it ground us
And be thankful for another day

You don't need to take a part of me
Because you're already complete
And you know yourself
Yes you know your worth

And I just want you to shine your light on me
Illuminate the divine in me
So we can be
Perfectly
The purest perfect forms of our uncapped potentiality

And I'll be bright
A shining light
Illuminating you in the darkest night

The purest energy
That's filling me and
In me already
Complete symbiotically

We all have our perfect purpose
And we all have our part to play

And we can go so deep still connected to the surface
And be thankful for another day

I'm in thanks for your brilliance
I'm in thanks for your divinity
And I know that the light that shines from you
Is the same that shines from me

I'm in complete acceptance of your beauty
And I know that you see that in me
My truest wish for your highest good
And your truest wish for me to fly free

The Faith Of Our Love

I know that midnight comes for us all
But you can always see the stars
Coldness and darkness may surround us all
But you will always feel comfort

Because I'll love you until the end of time
Yes I will always love you

I know that hardship may come to us all
But you'll always live in abundance
Trials and turmoil may always befall
But you'll always come through to your bliss

Because I'll love you until the end of time
Yes I will always love you

I will love you until the end of time
Yes I will always love you

I know that there may be falls along the way
But you will always get back up
There may be troubles that gets in the way
But you will always find a way through

Because I'll love you until the end of time
Yes I will always love you

I will love you until the end of time
Yes I will always love you

You know that no matter what may occur
You'll be smiling in the comfort of love
You know that anything sent to deter
Will never deter you from us

You'll love me until the end of time
Yes you will always love me

Because no matter what happens to us
We are free in the faith of our love

I Am Love

"I am Love" said the voice

"I wish to experience myself"

"Everything is energy"

"Everything is connected"

"Everything is one"

"Everything is all"

"Everything is spirit"

"Everything is Love"

"Everything has its perfect purpose"

"Everything is Divine"

"For something to know what it is"

"It must know what it is not"

"Hence relativity"

"The journey with its endless tries"

"To remember what you are"

"What all is"

"There is no judgement"

"There is only love"

"I am Love" said the voice

"And I love you"

Eternal Optimist

When surrounded by thorns I look for the rose
When the taste is bitter I appreciate the contrast that will enliven the
sweet
When it's raining I feel the cleanse of each drop
I see chains and envisage security
A thousand knives are pointed
So I look for a potato
A fire is spreading and I bask in it's glow
There's a dark tunnel so I anticipate the the light at its end
A window of light to enjoy
While others are looking at all of the turmoil
I am finding the joy
A shattered window from a stray ball
Brings me the thought of children playing freely outside
And the glazer that will have a new purpose
A new window that will let in more light
Trudging through a swamp
And I stop to feel
The softness of the mud on my skin
A swarm of wasps
Must be close to some honey
Wrapped up in drama
When I am playing
Fighting when I embrace
Shouting when I am singing
Falling when I have my grace
A child may be given by their parent
But to find the most gracious of arms
I see the expanse of the bliss
When others are fixated on the harm
When the world is imprisoned in fear
I see nature have a party outside
What may bring a person a tear
I sit and I smile instead
Because whatever bad thing you can witness
There is always a good thing in its stead

A Love Like This

Baby when I see you I know
You're my every wish
There is nothing I wouldn't do
For a love like this

Baby
For a love like this

And I'll be trying, I'll be trying, I'll be trying
Just to get back to you
And I'd be crying, I'd be lying if I didn't say I'm flying
Straight home to you

Baby
For a love like this

And the moon may fall from the sky
The world burst into flames
I would shelter you from the fire
And lift the moon up again

And the walls may come crashing down
From the sides of the safe
And the plates may shatter to the ground
But I'll keep you safe

Cause there is nothing there is nothing there is nothing
That I wouldn't do

Baby
For a love like this

And the rain may fall for days on end
And the seas all flood the land
But I'll never stop being your very best friend

And holding your hand

And the wind may blow the town away
Cars turned up on their sides
But I'll whisk you away on a speedy escape
To somewhere where it's alright

And I'll be trying, I'll be trying, I'll be trying
Just to get back to you
And I'd be'd crying, I'd be lying if I didn't say I'm flying
Straight home to you

Baby
For a love like this

You're my heart, you're my soul, you're my reason to evolve
You're my every wish
And the softness of your touch, and the kindness in your heart
Brings me a love like this

Baby, a love like this
There is nothing I wouldn't do
Baby for a love like this

I Thought

I thought I had so many
Thoughts and aspirations
I thought I had so many
Places that I must get to
I thought I had so many
Answers and further questions
I thought I had so many
Things that I must do

When I get there
And once I've done that
When I've past that hurdle
And once I get back

I thought I had so many
Thoughts and aspirations
A thirst to do it all
In every way on every nation
I want to save the world
But is that wasting my creation?
Is that just painting clouds
So that I can shine upon them?

Who am I to question
All of creation?
Edges of universes
And all expansion
It's all knowable
But not yet known by me
How do I know that
Everything's not exactly

As it's meant to be
As it's meant to be
As it's meant to be

As it's meant to be

The highest good for all
Expanding constantly
More of perfectness
Perfecting perfectly

I thought I had so many
Thoughts and aspirations

When I get there
Once I've let go of that
Once I learn the how tos
Stretch out to come back

Now I understand that
Letting go of old beliefs
Can bring me to new joy
Observe humbly, find peace
And yes I understand
More than I did yesterday
But yet I know there's vastness
That I can't anticipate

Now I feel comfortable
With leaving it up to
The happenings unravelling
That managed to get you

Human beings
To start being
Humans being
Kind to each other

Pioneers
Creators
Adventurers
And lovers

We're already here
In this moment now
I smile from ear to ear
The only word is wow

I don't need to look
Too far in to the future
I've got everything
That I need right here

All the knowledge
That I need to do the
Next best thing
That is already clear

I let go of the past
And thank it for its lessons
No concern for the future
I have faith in its blessings

Connect into the way
That I feel right now
The next best thing to do
Is where I put my out

All that you'll ever need
Is safe inside of you
Just watch those constant seeds
Grow in to their bloom

So sit contently
And witness humanity
Nature, creativity
Appreciating humbly

Kindly
Kindly
Kindly

I'm Home

I cross the road to go from the shade
In to the sunshine
And I feel fine

The bad things gone and left behind
Allowed me to make up my mind
And I'm excited for what I might find
What I might find

Can't change what's behind

I look forward
And feel the warmth of my sweater
I choose to be optimistic
Because it feels better

I wait at the crossing
For my turn to go
But if I just walked out and went with the flow
Who knows who knows?

Optimism carried me here
Set my intention and watch it appear
That confirmation I just about hear
Came through to me but not through my ears

A workman's off to work on a Sunday
But what days of rest are left for my fun days
Cold chills in the air but I've got the sun rays

I'm happy here not searching for my place

I'm home

I'm home, I'm home
I'm home, I'm home

Channelled Consciousness

I write this as a vessel of source
Not opinionated but bestowed with the knowledge that flows from me, within me
Only ever from a place of love
Guided by love and instructed by love
The understanding that no being is ever born or created from a place of evil or hate
That only love will overcome all eventualities
A human only needs to experience the birth of humanity
To then understand that no soul can ever enter the world in any other place other than love
That no matter where a soul has come it has always come from love
There are many influences that will lead and impose upon us
There is much information available but no matter what,
No matter how far from the source one may stray the core of love will always remain
What you see or dictate as opinion will be your creation of another
But that other is pure in soul regardless of their position in their journey
Your perception of them is yours and therefore your creation of what or where they are
It is human infallibility that leads to negative perception
If only we are to give all beings complete love then the best version of each being will be
Each soul empowered to create their own being
And version of themselves both spiritually and physically
Perception of the being is completely created in the eye of the beholder
There will be times, for some many, for some rarely
But for all times when we will be disconnected
I believe that we are close to if not already embarked upon an age of love
No matter where humanity is, what culture, what background
Upbringing, race, creed, faith, knowledge base, sexual orientation etc
Underlying in every category you could associate with another
In any way is the essence of individuality and the essence of together-ness

We are all built from pure love
It is contained in us
It flows to us, through us and from us
Some call it source energy, some life force, some chi and many other names
I call it love
It is the pure energy that is at the heart of all beings everywhere
Those that are led down the wrong path may do so through disconnection
But yet are still always connected and so eventually the love will overcome
In this lifetime, or a future lifetime
If only a human is to feel the complete love which is ever present
They could not do anything with any evil or malicious intent
We are a world of geniuses, each in our own way
It was Einstein that said if you judge a fish on its ability to climb trees
It will spend it's life thinking it's an idiot
I am here to comfortably say that no being is an idiot
We are all equally divine
Find the divine in you, believe in it and it will be
Bold and bright for all to see

Judge Me

Judge me
For being different and weird
And that my jokes might offend

But I'm not here to please
And try and make friends

I've got all that I need

My crew, My click, our creed
All of them great
All a different breed

And in hard times
When look around and see
All of your mates are not there
But mine stood by me
Then you'll know what I mean

Stood through the test of time
The dirt and the grime
And all of them I still call mine

Not one of them has ever gave up on me
All of them relentless
Even when withdrawn from rest

And furthermore
We seem to thrive off each other's success
And I can honestly say
All of you are my best

They're the kind of breed

That are kind without need
Let you through the gates open armed
But won't be brought to their knees

And they do as they please
Which often at times
Is to help others achieve

So please

Now you understand them, understand me
To be in the presence of their greatness
What man must I be?

To be defended at all times
By these great giants
Not one of them ever to change alliance

And not through blindness
But the ability to see
That the greatness of the universe
Flows through me

And when you remove the blinds
And cast judgement away
So you can see true
You'll see that I'm great

By finally recognising
The greatness in you

By James Hayes

Found

I watch as my reflection bares a jubilant smile that catches my heart
It wails in bliss as I focus on the stream of sunlight creating dark bodies
of art
I simply am not able to tame my joyous mind as it climbs the chart
It pierced the boundary of virtue like a tapered trident dart
I believe my momentous mind is one that will never become absent and
never depart

Everything in this landscape of tranquility bares a story of great
The still silence fills my mind with roaring sound that raises my heart
rate

The abyss the sun's child brings during nightfall carries my hope in
freight

The secrecy and concealment allows my mind to truly unlatch the gate
I see through the cracks of the heftiest cells and when anger arises I
negate

The racing introspection of my mind chases me like a hound
That same hound is the one that pushed me to eminence and caused
me to be crowned
The same thing that allowed me to fly also bound me to the ground
It saved me from the thunder storms that were upper bound
And from there on I was found

Autumn

The bleak, brisk autumn breath rustled withered leaves of the insipid tree
The cruel, crisp bite of the wind devoured my finger as I trod through the orange leaf sea
The sun hung low in the murky sky and the clouds latched to the horizon
I got lost in my thoughts and the dull hum of silence
And I reminisced all the times and all the joy of life
I realised the selection of bliss was plentiful, even rife

Then I thought of the tough times, the trove of memories
Surely these scars could be cured, was there a medicine, a remedy?
Then I looked again in a new light and I changed
Instead of hurt and pain, think of all the advice that life let you obtain
All the times you were happy, kind, blessed, entertained
Think of all the experience and wisdom you've obtained.
Wow

Think from the right window
Don't look at the clouds
Look at the sun between them
Think of all of the wonderful things that you have overcome
Glass half empty, glass half full
Which will it be?
Everything is blessed, good and wonderful to some degree
It's not the situation that's bad it's your vision
If I could only see life that way I would keep my eyes closed
That's my decision

The rife autumn whisper rustled the lush, lavish leaves of the flourishing tree
The caring love of the wind soothed my mind as I swam through the orange leaf sea

The sun came close to kiss the clouds that were greeting the tip of the horizon
I experienced love in the soothing hum of silence
And I reminisced all the times and all the joy of life
I realised the selection of bliss was plentiful, even rife

No. Yes. No.

No.
Yes.
No.
Consider their implications.
Weighty words
Fishbait leaden complications.
Simply constructed
But such heavy considerations.
The soft flesh of dreams
Shimmering in uncertainty
Bones into a grin of realisation
Or, softens further
And releases its grip on what might be.
Grows flaccid.
An amoeba of tears
Spreading its false feet
Nervously moving to grip and feed
But finding nothing,
Spreading more thinly until nothing itself.
So, a relationship begins
With a "Yes" and a "No".
Simply constructed
And simply destroyed

Written in his twenties

Reflections In The Varnish

Searching through the magazines
For photographs of someone to love.
The rain has speckled them.

I tripped and fell most awkwardly:
Impossible black shapes from out beyond the ferry
Reflections in the varnish.
A Japanese flower in a garden
Changed somehow,
It's hard to tell through the grey glass of evening.

Another face, another way.
The sounds drift in drowning,
Like those frantic thoughts just before sleep.
The crackling radio of another world.

So strange to see her that way.
My hand reached up to her.
All the moments of electricity
And her obsession with tomorrow.

Pick up your coins young lady
You caused me to thank you.

I could wish…

I could wish for a modern kitchen all decked out in Stiffkey blue
I could wish for a dark green Jaguar that's shiny, bright and new
I could wish for a forest cabin with the sunlight streaming through
I could wish for a cottage garden lightly jewelled with morning dew
I could wish for sun baked days in Venice Beach or Malibu
I could wish for gourmet dinners with a glass of wine or two
I could wish for breezy Cornish walks with a sparkling ocean view
I could wish for oak beamed country pubs and pints of foaming brew
I could wish to have my name in lights or in DeBrett's Who's Who
I could wish that all my golf shots flew off steady, straight and true
I could wish, Yes, I could wish
But all I really want, is you.

For Larkin

Inside this life, as now, I find so many steps that lie behind.
They're what they are and can't be changed, reinvented, rearranged.
The people I have loved and known, like many tumbling dice were thrown
across a cloth of chance and fate, hope and fear, love and hate
to make adventures of their own, blithely forged and formed and grown
built on trust and faith and ties, promises and truth and lies.
And where they go and what they'll be, matters not to you and me.
Each life's a journey to we know not where. All we know is that we're going there!
And when in bed, I lie quite dead, I hope these gentle words be read:
No taste, no sound, no smell, no eyes, no touch to welcome my demise.
No reason to philosophise, eternal darkness is my prize.

For Margaret

We gather here from far and near
Upon this bridge above the weir
With its gentle susurration
And hushed green tree congregation
Two sisters tall and strong in grief
Let ashes fall in stream so brief
That shimmers like the silver sand
White roses tumble from each hand
Into the river wide and deep
We all entrust it now to keep
The memories of one we knew
All different yet, not one less true
Muma, Nana or dearest friend
Who lived life full right to the end
We thank you for your greatest gift
How to live a life well lived.

A wish

Letting the living deal with the dying
Isn't a lot of fun!
It is better to quietly slip into shadow
While children play in the sun.
It is wrong that the dead can torture the living
And steal away their time
Let them glory in all that they love in their lives
And not grieve for the end of mine.

For his children

Final note:

To my parents. Thank you. For all you have done. For us and others and for the world around you. For all that is. For the lessons, the consideration, the comfort, the safety, the support, the sacrifices, the acceptance, the soft guidance, the love, the truth and the lies. You are pure, kind, inspirational beings. Massively influential whilst giving absolute freedom to choose, discover, decide, make mistakes and walk our own paths. My wish is that Sophie and I can be to our children what you have been to us. I love you so much.

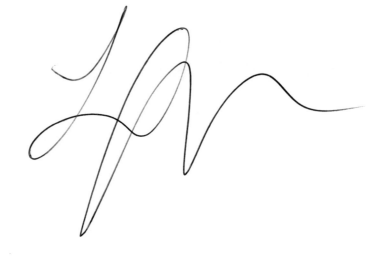

To Mikey,

My Brother!

Thanks so much
for buying my book.
Means a lot!

You're a legend bro.
Big love for you and
Lauren & all the
joy you've bought
to my life. Some
of my very favourite
people. Lots of love. Luke
xxx

Lightning Source UK Ltd.
Milton Keynes UK
UKHW020640031120
372717UK00011B/667